George Allen

A Senator Speaks Out on Liberty, Opportunity *and* Security

MODERN AMERICAN STATESMAN SERIES

★ ★ ★

M

MONUMENT
PRESS

George Allen:
A Senator Speaks Out On Liberty, Opportunity, and Security
by Monument Press

Printed in the United States of America

ISBN 0-9769668-1-6

601 Pennsylvania Avenue, N.W.
Suite 900, South Building
Washington D.C., 20004
202-220-3195

www.MonumentPress.org

A NOTE FROM THE PUBLISHER

Monument Press is proud to present the *Modern American Statesmen Series*. This series offers the best in public speeches and remarks given by our most prominent elected officials. All the material in the series was originally spoken from the floors of the U.S. House of Representatives and the U.S. Senate.

Throughout American history, members of Congress have given important speeches and remarks from the floors of the House and Senate. From Senator Thomas Jefferson's floor discourses on Federalism to Senator John F. Kennedy's floor speeches on Civil Rights to Senator Richard Nixon's floor lectures on communism, they constituted the fundamental nature of public opinion and public discourse of their time.

Today, during hearings, debates, and floor proceedings, members of Congress still weigh issues of monumental national importance. We believe their words should be published and distributed in a manner that is accessible to the general public. The material herein gives the reader the best thoughts of United States senators and representatives. It sheds light on the past, present, and future of the nation's laws and policies, covering issues of war and peace, taxation, education, national security, general welfare, health and social security, morality, and others.

The speeches in this book will be found authentic and accurate. They are published as spoken and recorded by Congress. As such, some of the grammar, syntax, and sentence structure may not conform to normal editorial styles. The words are published just as they were spoken.

The *Modern American Statesmen Series* is a non-partisan project. We aim to give the reader the mere truth about what's been spoken on the floors of the House and Senate, with no commentary or observation.

The series is compiled and edited by Bryan T. Mullican, Senior Editor of Monument Press. An editor, researcher and award-winning journalist, Mullican previously served as a Research Analyst for the Republican National Committee during the 2004 Presidential Campaign and also as Managing Editor of *The Tower* newspaper at The Catholic University of America.

Thomas M. Freiling
Publisher, Monument Press
Washington, D.C.

TABLE OF CONTENTS

"Excessive taxation limits the individual freedom of hard-working Americans, their families, and their enterprises. ... It is common sense—trusting families, trusting people. They know better than the Federal Government about what they need and how to make their earnings work for themselves, their families, and their enterprises."

TAX REFORM

February 8, 2001

Mr. President, I rise to state that Americans need tax relief and I believe they need it now. Despite record economic growth for the last several years, and huge budgeted surpluses in the last few years and in the future, I think these surpluses simply represent overtaxation of the American taxpayers. Americans, in recent years, have been repeatedly denied tax relief despite these surpluses because there were not enough Senators to override the President's veto—the previous President's veto.

Excessive taxation limits the individual freedom of hard-working Americans, their families, and their enterprises. I agree very much with the previous remarks made by the Senator from Arizona, Mr. Kyl, and the Senator from Missouri, Mr. Bond.

The fact is, Americans are paying more in taxes as a proportion of the gross domestic product than at any time since World War II. In fact, for this fiscal year, the Federal Government will pull out $1 of every $5 in the economy—20 percent of the economy is being taken by the Federal Government, even though there is a non-Social Security budget surplus in this year that is going to top $125 billion, and it is going to exceed $3.1 trillion over the next decade.

I believe we must assure that Americans can keep more of their hard-earned dollars in their pockets. Previously, the Senator from Connecticut paraphrased a song to slow down tax cuts in this surplus. I think there is a more apt country western song to reference this gold mine surplus that is created by the work of the taxpayers. What has been suggested by the opponents is that the Government gets the gold mines and the taxpayers get the shaft.

I think the taxpayers deserve better. It is simply common sense that, rather than continuing down the path of excessive Government spending in Washington, Americans ought to be allowed more money to invest in their priorities for their families, for their homes: saving for retirement or the purchase of a computer for their children. It is common sense—trusting families, trusting people. They know better than the Federal Government about what they need and how to make their earnings work for themselves, their families, and their enterprises.

Overall, for the economic success and jobs in America, I believe the Federal Reserve needs to rapidly reduce interest rates much more, and soon; we must pass tax relief soon to help bolster consumer confidence. When you look at these surpluses, I believe they ought to be handled the same way a well-managed business would handle surpluses. A business would first put funds into retirement or pension funds. Then they would look at their priorities as a company and invest in them. And then they would look for a dividend to the shareholders.

As the Federal Government, I think we ought to look at it the same way a business would. Certainly a business would not be raiding, at times of surplus—or at any time for that matter—pension funds or retirement funds. That is why I think as a Government we need to protect Social Security. Put Social Security in a lockbox. Hopefully, with this spirit of bipartisanship, that will change and we can pass legislation necessary to protect Social Security so future retirement funds are not raided for more Government spending.

The advantage of the Social Security lockbox is not only protection of retirement funds; it also helps pay down the national debt. Implementing the Social Security lockbox and allowing those surpluses to be used only for addressing the long-term solvency of Social Security helps us reduce the national debt, and we can effectively eliminate the publicly held debt in the next 10 years with that fiscal discipline.

Then I believe we need to look at the non-Social Security surpluses and, again, handle it the same way a well-run business would. What would a well-run business do with the non-retirement surpluses? They would address priorities, research and development, workforce training, maybe investment in ideas to be more competitive, or increase their market share. In the Federal Government, even after we save and protect the Social Security surpluses and pay down the national debt, the Federal Government still will be collecting $3.1 trillion more in taxes than is needed at the current levels of spending, on top of the current level of spending inflationary increases. So it is $3.1 trillion. That is over $10,000 of excess taxation of every man, woman, and child in this country.

There are legitimate national responsibilities we need to address and in which we need to invest. We must provide that out of this $3.1 trillion surplus. There are new investments we need to consider in education. We must also act quickly, making sure we are improving the preparedness of our national defense and our Armed Forces. We need to invest in new technological and scientific research. We need to shore up the Medicare system, as well as investing in our national transportation infrastructure.

But once we take care of these priority responsibilities in education, national defense, scientific research, and combating illegal drug trade, we should again operate as a business. Then what would a business do after you take care of priorities? They would declare a dividend. That is what I think we ought to do is declare a dividend for the shareholders, the owners of this Government who are the taxpayers of America.

Surely, out of the $3.1 trillion surplus, I do not think the $1.6 trillion the Bush administration is proposing is an excessive amount to return to our taxpayers. It is a minimal amount we ought to be returning to the taxpayers. In fact, when you compare this proposal to previous major tax cuts, history shows we can dedicate even 50 percent of the current non-Social Security surplus to tax relief measures and still barely make a blip on the radar screen of our national economy.

For example, in 1963 President Kennedy's tax cut reduced tax collections by 12 percent. That is this chart here, the Kennedy administration; it was 12.6 percent.

The Reagan administration 1981 tax cut reduced tax collections by 18.7 percent—nearly 19 percent.

The tax collections proposed by the Bush administration would return just over one-half of the excess tax collections to American taxpayers, and the tax collections would be reduced by 6.2 percent—much less than the Kennedy and much less than the Reagan administrations. In fact, according to the National Taxpayers' Union, as part of our gross domestic product, when you compare the Kennedy tax cut, it was 2 percent of the gross domestic product—the Bush proposal of taxes being reduced by $1.6 trillion is a mere 1.2 percent of the gross domestic product.

You might recall the great growth in our economy in the 1960s was occasioned by the tax cuts of the Kennedy administration. So this is merely one-half of the revenue impact of the Kennedy tax cut.

I say to my colleagues in the Senate, if we cannot cut taxes in the times of these surpluses, when will we be able to give tax relief and reduce the tax burden on the people of America?

This is the time to make the Federal Tax Code more fair and less burdensome. This is the time to get rid of this illogical marriage penalty tax which imposes a penalty on men and women just because they are married. This is the time to eliminate the death tax which is a very unfair tax, especially on family farms and small businesses. This is the time to make sure that individuals and small business owners get 100-percent tax deductibility for health insurance. And there are many other things we can do. This is the time to act for the people of America.

I hope my Senate colleagues will seize this opportunity to exercise fiscal discipline and restraint and realize that the owners of this country deserves tax relief, and they deserve it now.

[Congressional Record: S1175]

January 29, 2002

Mr. President, I commend Senator Sessions for his leadership and echo all of the comments he made in support of this measure. I strongly support, as a cosponsor, this amendment which is entitled the American Family Economic Security and Stimulus Act.

This amendment, due to the great leadership of Senator Sessions, as well as his ingenuity, has provided us with what I believe to be a very common sense, compassionate, pro-family package that will help stimulate the economy and help American families and businesses get through the current economic recession.

When one thinks of stimulus or stimulus policy—I know the Presiding Officer remembers the discussion on the concept of stimulus—it should be a change in policy which will induce or spur economic activity, whether it is investment or whether it is spending, that would otherwise not occur but for the change in policy.

This amendment represents a very worker-oriented, pro-family economic aid and stimulus package that will provide immediate financial relief to working families. It will ensure more of their hard-earned money stays in their wallets, and they spend it as they see fit. There is the additional $150 a month in the hands of working Americans through advanced payment on the earned-income tax credit. That is really an immediate 50 to 60 cents per hour pay raise for workers in the lowest income levels.

It increases the child tax credit to $1,000 for the current fiscal year, and it accelerates the rate reduction for the 28 percent tax bracket to 25 percent.

I thank Senator Sessions for including the educational opportunity tax credit in this important legislation. This is a concept that I ran on in my campaign. It is one many have heard me discuss. What I am doing in adapting this idea, the education opportunity tax credit, to a stimulus package is to create an immediate incentive for families, parents of children who are in kindergarten through 12th grade, to buy computers, educational software, or computer peripherals. It is a technology-related amendment.

Specifically, what this amendment, the Sessions-Allen amendment, would do is provide parents who have children in kindergarten through 12th grade with an immediate $2,500 tax credit to buy computers, educational software, or peripherals. It would be for only 3 months. It would provide those families with the financial means necessary to provide their children with greater educational choice and opportunities best suited to their individual needs.

Parents know the needs of their children better than anyone. We know in studies about the digital divide that youngsters who have computers at home do better in school. They stay in school. They don't drop out. This is an important way of empowering parents to provide computers and educational software and peripherals to their children.

As far as the economic stimulus of it, if the idea of education and empowering parents is not sufficient to convince my colleagues, let's recognize what this will do for the economy. We can look at the States as our laboratories for a lot of good ideas.

Experience shows in the States that even a small temporary reduction in taxes can bring about huge increases in computer sales. In South Carolina, they had a sales tax holiday on computers for only 3 days. What was the result? Computer sales increased more than tenfold, over 1,000 percent, in those 3 days. In Pennsylvania, they eliminated the sales tax on computers for 1 week. CPU sales increased six fold in that time. ...

Mr. President, I hope the Senate will support this idea of empowering parents, helping with technology, and helping out our economy as well. It is a good, commonsense approach. I thank the Presiding Officer for giving me the additional 30 seconds.

[Congressional Record: S211-212]

"I cannot ever envision a time when it will be okay for any government to tax freedom on the Internet by taxing access to the Internet. ... Furthermore, the more expensive you make Internet access, the less likely people are to buy advanced services, including broadband delivered high-speed Internet access, multimedia expansion cards, and Internet protocol enabling software."

INTERNET TAX FREEDOM

October 10, 2001

Mr. President, I rise today to introduce the Defense of Internet Tax Freedom Act, with my friends and colleagues from California, Montana, New Hampshire, and Virginia, to extend the moratorium on Internet access taxes and multiple and discriminatory taxes for five-years. As you know, the original provisions of the Internet Tax Freedom Act are set to expire this October 21, less than two weeks from now.

As many in this chamber know, I have made extending the moratorium on taxes that discriminate against the Internet one of my top priorities since coming to the Senate. I cannot ever envision a time when it will be okay for any government to tax freedom on the Internet by taxing access to the Internet. I cannot ever conceive of any instance or event that will precipitate justification for multiple or discriminatory taxes on the Internet by any government, large or small, national or local.

For this reason, I have maintained constant and steady support for the permanent extension of the Internet moratorium on Internet access, multiple and discriminatory taxes. I never thought I would be willing to vote for, much less sponsor, legislation that endorsed a limited extension, but the events of September 11, 2001 have forced all of us in this Congress, and indeed throughout the country, to think and act according to the most immediate interests of our Nation.

Now, more than ever, the people of this country need security, not only with regard to safety, but also with regard to their financial future. Any additional tax burdens on the Internet now, will mean additional costs that many Americans cannot afford, forcing the poorest in our society to reduce or even forgo their use of the Internet as a tool for education and exploration.

Consider the fact that by taxing Internet access, States and localities are actually contributing to an already growing economic "digital divide." For every dollar added to the cost of Internet access, we can expect to see lost utilization of the Internet by thousands of poor and impoverished families nationwide.

Furthermore, the more expensive you make Internet access, the less likely people are to buy advanced services, including broadband delivered high-speed Internet access, multimedia expansion cards, and Internet protocol enabling software. Given the current state of the technology market as a whole, a decrease in consumption resulting from Internet access taxes could destroy what glimmer of hope remains for many telecommunications and technology manufacturers.

The effects of these closures have already been felt throughout our country. Congress should be working to keep businesses open and Americans employed, and that is why we must pass a reasonable extension of the moratorium on Internet access, multiple, and discriminatory taxes.

If you consider for a moment that the Internet has only been around in its contemporary form since 1995 or 1996, then you realize that this technology and the impact it has made and will continue to make on our economy is both very promising and very unsure. To date we have very little reliable data as to the real impact the Internet is making on the daily lives of Americans.

We have little to no information as to how and why consumers on the web decide to spend their hard earned money. We have no real evidence that consumers would decide to spend money or purchase products they buy on the web today if these products were only available in traditional brick-n-mortar settings.

The studies we have seen thus far all contradict one another. In one study dealing with the effects of Internet purchasing on State revenues, I found a quote from the President of the National Conference of State Legislatures comparing State budgets in recent years to the engine of a luxury car. Yet, I have heard from this and other organizations that the Internet is destroying State tax revenue streams.

I don't know who or what to believe. All I know is that many in this Senate need time to understand this issue. There are many members in this body who do not fully recognize that the moratorium is completely unrelated to sales taxes or the collection thereof. Given that fact, I cannot see why extending the moratorium for a mere few months or years would be beneficial in terms of educating the general public and the Members of this body.

In a matter of months or a few years, the technology sector will only just be at the point of full recovery from the current downturn in our economy. We will need several years beyond that point of full recovery to complete the comprehensive, neutral studies of the Internet and e-commerce that Members of Congress will need in order to make these important decisions, decisions that may directly challenge the conventional wisdom of our Founding Fathers and our own historical experience.

Given these requirements, five years seems to be the minimum amount of time Congress, the private sector, and other interested organizations will need in order to make well-informed, proactive decisions regarding other issues not related to the Internet moratorium.

In the meantime, we can guarantee a level of stability for the Internet over the next five years that will allow our Nation to continue to close the digital divide and encourage new and enhanced uses of the web for consumers.

I call on my colleagues to join me and my fellow cosponsors in cosponsoring the Defense of Internet Tax Freedom Act, in supporting a five year extension of the Internet moratorium on access multiple and discriminatory taxes.

Let's give the Internet the future it deserves and show America that the answer is not more taxes but rather better, more efficient government for the people and by the people.

[Congressional Record: S10459-10460]

January 13, 2003

Mr. President, today I rise to introduce the Internet Tax Nondiscrimination Act of 2003, to permanently extend the moratorium on Internet access taxes, as well as prevent multiple and discriminatory taxes on the Internet. There are two postulates in life that guide me today: first, always stand strong for freedom and opportunity for all people; and second, always keep your word and keep your promises.

As many in this chamber know, I have made permanently extending the moratorium on new taxes that discriminate against the Internet one of my top priorities since coming to the Senate. Looking back two years ago, as a rookie, I was pleased to work in the successful effort, with Senator McCain and others, to extend the moratorium on new Internet taxes for two years. Of course, I would have preferred to have a permanent moratorium and introduced S. 777 to do so back in 2001.

I cannot ever envision a time when it will be desirable policy for any government to tax access to the Internet. I cannot ever conceive of any instance or event that will precipitate justification for multiple or discriminatory taxes on the Internet by any government, large or small, national, State or local.

This has been a position I have held from 1997 during my days as Governor of Virginia when I was one of only four Governors with this position. I have promised the first bill I'd introduce in the 108th Congress would be a permanent ban on discriminatory taxes and Internet access taxes. I am one who stands on the side of freedom of the Internet, trusting free people and entrepreneurs, not on the side of making this advancement in technology easier to tax for the tax collectors. My legislation will permanently ban taxes on Internet access, as well as taxes on Internet transactions by multiple jurisdictions, and discriminatory taxes that unfairly target Internet transactions.

The current moratorium on Internet tax is set to expire in November of this year. I want the members of this body to understand that the moratorium on Internet tax is completely unrelated to issues surrounding sales tax simplification. I was here for the previous debate when legislation extending this moratorium was bogged down and held hostage on the extremely complicated and cumbersome issue of sales tax collection.

Since that time, I know State tax administrators have been working to simplify their sales tax system. However, I encourage my colleagues in the Senate that when considering the issue of sales tax simplification and business activity tax nexus that they do so separately from legislation that deals with the Internet tax moratorium.

I understand most of the States are looking for more tax revenue, but the Internet Tax Nondiscrimination Act will not, and does not, prohibit States from collecting sales and use tax on electronic commerce. Rather, this legislation will permanently ban taxes placed on consumers to access the Internet, like the Spanish American War Tax on telephone service, and prohibits multiple and discriminatory taxes on Internet purchases, which are taxes that would apply more than once on the same product or taxes that are higher because of the method by which a product is purchased.

The moratorium on Internet access taxes prohibits governments from placing taxes on top of the monthly rates Americans already pay to connect to the Internet. I am concerned that if this Congress were to allow new, discriminatory taxes on Internet access it would be allowing States and localities to contribute to the economic "digital divide." For every dollar added to the cost of Internet access, we can expect to see lost utilization of the Internet by thousands of lower income American families nationwide.

Now, more than ever, with our Nation's economy emerging from a recession and the Congress working with the President on an economic stimulus package, the people of this country need security with regard to their financial future. Any additional tax burdens on the Internet, will mean additional costs that many Americans cannot afford, forcing the poorest in our society to reduce or even forgo their use of the Internet as a tool for education, exploration and individual opportunity.

The more expensive the government makes Internet access, the less likely people will be to buy advanced services, such as high-speed broadband connections, Internet protocol software, wireless WiFi devices and many other multimedia applications. In a time when technology and the Internet have grown into every aspect of our daily lives and where access to the Internet has become a necessity for Americans, will imposing taxes to access the Internet or levying taxes that discriminate against the Internet as a form of commerce ever be fair? The answer is that there will never be a time to tax access to the Internet nor impose discriminatory taxes on Internet commerce.

The goal of the Internet Tax Nondiscrimination Act is simple and clear: the Internet should remain as accessible as possible to all people in all parts of our country, forever.

I call on my colleagues to join me and cosponsor the Internet Tax Nondiscrimination Act of 2003, permanently extending the Internet moratorium on access, multiple and discriminatory taxes.

[Congressional Record: S236]

November 3, 2003

Mr. President, I rise today to ask my colleagues to support S. 150, the Internet Tax Nondiscrimination Act.

As many of my colleagues have heard me say on many occasions, I believe it is important that we—and I tried to do it myself—advocate policies and ideas that promote freedom and opportunity for all Americans. We in the Senate must advance ideas that help create more investment, thereby creating more jobs and prosperity rather than more burdens from taxation and regulation.

This measure permanently extends the moratorium banning access taxes and taxes that discriminate against the Internet. It is one of my priorities. I know the Senator presiding shares that same philosophy and has been a great leader in that regard.

As we all know, the Internet is one of our country's greatest tools and symbols of innovation and individual empowerment. I look at the invention of the Internet as profoundly transforming and revolutionary for the dissemination of ideas and information, as important as was the Gutenberg Press.

Accordingly, I think everyone in the Senate would want to help the Internet grow and flourish as a viable tool for education, information, and commerce. I stand on the side of freedom of the Internet, trusting free people and free entrepreneurs—not on the side of making this advancement in technology easier to tax for the tax collectors.

One of the great things about the Internet is that it is not limited by boundaries of State governments, local governments, not even limited by the boundary of this country. Clearly, the Internet is intrastate commerce. Thus, the Federal Government, Congress, has jurisdiction in the taxation and regulation of the Internet.

My legislation, S. 150, promotes equal access to the Internet for all Americans and protects every American from harmful, regressive taxes on Internet access services as well as duplicative and predatory taxes on Internet transactions. Specifically, as reported out of the Commerce Committee, S. 150 has five provisions.

First, it extends permanently the country's Federal prohibition of State and local taxation on Internet access service.

Second, it makes permanent the ban on all multiple and discriminatory taxes relating to electronic commerce. This ensures that several jurisdictions cannot tax the same transaction simply because the transaction happens to occur over the Internet.

Third, my legislation repeals the so-called grandfathering provision over a 3-year-period.

Fourth, we make clear the original intent of the Internet Tax Freedom Act by updating the definition of Internet access to ensure the moratorium applies consistently to all consumers. If we are going to exempt Internet access services from taxation permanently, then it makes sense to do so in a manner that applies to all methods and ways a consumer might have access to the Internet, regardless of how they choose to access it, whether by DSL—digital subscriber line connections—by wireless connections, by cable modem service, satellite, or dial-up service.

Fifth, and lastly, this legislation ensures that nothing prevents the collection or remittance of State and Federal universal service fees.

The Internet tax moratorium has contributed to extending Internet access to over 127 million citizens, approximately 45 percent of our country's population. Unfortunately, that moratorium expired Friday night. Every day that the moratorium lapses, consumers are susceptible to more pestering, burdensome new taxes on Internet access services, as well as taxes on e-mail, taxes on instant messages, spam filters, and even Web searches.

For every dollar in taxation—and most kids in elementary school will understand these economics—every dollar added in taxation adds to the cost of the Internet access. With that, you could expect to see lost utilization of the Internet by thousands of American families, especially lower income families.

According to the Pew Internet and American Life Project, 30 percent of non-internet users say cost is the major reason they remain off line. Additionally, 43 percent of non-internet users agreed with the statement, "Internet access is too expensive."

For roughly 55 percent of the American people who are still off line, keeping access affordable—and that means keeping access free from State, local, and Federal taxation—is vital.

The guiding principle of this legislation is simple and clear: The Internet should remain as accessible as possible to all people in all parts of the country forever. That has been the position I have taken on this and held since 1997 during my days as Governor of Virginia when I was one of only four Governors to share this position.

I cannot envision any time in our future where it will be desirable for any government to tax access to the Internet. I cannot envision any instance or event that would precipitate the justification for multiple or discriminatory taxes on the Internet by any government, whether large or small, local, State, or national.

Yet if the Senate fails to take action by the end of this week or any Senator votes against this legislation, such Member is in effect advocating taxing the Internet.

There are more Americans empowered by the Internet primarily because the Federal policy of the United States has consciously allowed Internet innovators, entrepreneurs, and consumers to remain free from onerous taxation.

As many know, Congress first enacted this moratorium with the Internet Tax Freedom Act in 1998 after dozens of State and local taxing commissars began to impose disparate taxes on a consumer's ability to access the Internet.

Since the last extension of the Internet Tax Freedom Act in 2001, some States have begun taxing the high-speed component of broadband Internet access services by asserting that certain portions of high-speed broadband Internet access are telecommunication services rather than Internet access services. The States doing this are therefore circumventing the original intentions of the law.

Working with our chairman of the Commerce Committee, Senator John McCain, as well as Senator Ron Wyden and Senator John Sununu in the Commerce Committee, we have updated the definition of Internet access to ensure that all Internet access services, regardless of the technology used to deliver that service, are covered by the moratorium and therefore exempt from State and local taxation.

I want to also address for my colleagues the misleading statements made regarding S. 150. I understand the proponents of higher taxes at the State and local level have raised a number of concerns about this legislation, indicating that we expanded the moratorium on Internet access to include all telecommunication services, making tax free even traditional services such as local and long-distance telephone communications. Additionally, they have raised the question whether or not this bill would prohibit States from imposing property and corporate income taxes on telecommunication carriers and Internet service providers. The false assertions come maybe from confusion, maybe from a misunderstanding, but in some cases they are intentionally, outright, and flat wrong statements. I am here to set the record straight.

I want all the Members of this body to understand and be clear on the facts about this legislation: S. 150 does not affect traditional voice or long-distance telephone services or any other communication service that is not directly used to provide Internet access; S. 150 does not affect a State's ability to collect income, property, or other corporate taxes, such as franchising fees, that are unrelated to Internet access.

The fact is S. 150 does not unnecessarily expand the moratorium on Internet access. Rather, the legislation clarifies the original intentions of the Internet Tax Freedom Act to include high-speed Internet access services. Only because some States and localities attempted to circumvent the original law by taxing portions of high-speed Internet access did the definition of Internet access need to be updated.

The impact of what the States and localities are trying to do in taxing broadband has implications that particularly are harmful to small communities and rural areas. We have always advocated that we have to get broadband to rural areas. Obviously, it costs a great deal of money. Our good colleague, Senator Conrad Burns, says out in the country there is a lot of dirt to dig between light bulbs.

If you are going to get broadband to rural areas, there is a great investment to get it there because you have a fewer number of customers to recoup your investment. In the event a tax is put on to broadband, it means obviously fewer people can afford it, thereby making it less likely that a company is going to invest the millions and millions of dollars it will take to get broadband deployed or high speed deployed to rural areas, thereby ruining, hindering, hampering the ability of people and small businesses in rural communities to get access to high-speed Internet services which is vital for them getting information, education, as well as conducting business.

The fact is, S. 150 only makes permanent the tax moratorium on Internet access services, which is simply the ability to get access to the Internet. Once a consumer has accessed the Internet, the moratorium does not affect the services that are purchased, used, or sold over the Internet that would otherwise be taxable, even if those services are bundled together with Internet access services.

Proponents of Internet taxes say this bill is an unfunded mandate. The fact is, the cost associated with S. 150 only affects those few States and localities that were grandfathered under the original Tax Freedom Act of 1998. Additionally, my legislation delays the repeal of the grandfathering provision for a 3-year period, ensuring that the moratorium on Internet access taxes applies equally in all 50 States, while giving these few taxing States and localities additional time to adjust their budgets accordingly.

Let's realize this has been now 5 years where these States and localities have had time—5 years—to remove these Internet access taxes. With my bill, S. 150, they will have, in effect, 8 years to repeal these regressive taxes on Internet access.

I would invite them to look at the record since the enactment of the 1998 moratorium where several States, plus the District of Columbia, have in fact chosen to move away from Internet taxes.

For example, in 1999, Iowa enacted a law specifically exempting Internet access from taxation. In South Carolina, after the enactment of the Federal moratorium in 1998, the Governor and tax department issued formal announcements indicating the State would abide by the national tax moratorium and would cease trying to collect taxes on Internet access services. Connecticut's State legislature approved a law that accelerated the phase-out of Internet access taxes in July of 2001. Additionally, in April of 2000, Arizona enacted a law exempting Internet access from State and local sales tax. Finally, in 1999, the District of Columbia also eliminated taxes on Internet access.

Meanwhile, we do have these other States—for example, Kentucky, Alabama, and others—that have attempted to tax the transport of high-speed broadband Internet access.

In summary, the fact is, by allowing the moratorium to expire, the Senate has opened the door for States and localities to begin imposing regressive taxes on Internet access services. By taxing Internet access, States and localities are actually contributing to the economic digital divide. The more expensive we allow the State and local tax commissars to make Internet access, the less likely people are to be able to buy these advanced services, such as high-speed broadband connections. It makes it harder for them to purchase Internet protocol software, wireless fidelity, or WiFi devices, or many other multimedia applications. These applications are all made less likely to be affordable for many millions of Americans.

In a time when technology and the Internet have grown into improving almost every aspect of our daily lives, and where access to the Internet is a necessity for Americans, it just seems to me that imposing new taxes on access or levying taxes that discriminate against the Internet as a form of commerce will just never be sound policy for our country.

As a tool, what is great about the Internet is it breaks down economic and educational barriers, leveling the playing field for millions of Americans.

You will also hear some say: Let's just have a short extension. Let's have a short extension. We do not need to make it permanent. Well, going back to the business model and understanding how businesses have to invest, they like to see some certainty. If you have a short moratorium, there is less certainty, there is less predictability for investment, therefore, fewer job opportunities, and less likelihood that broadband or high speed will get out to the smaller towns and communities in rural areas.

More than ever before, with our Nation's economy finally moving forward in the right direction, the people of this country need security with regard to their financial future. Any additional tax burdens on the Internet will mean additional costs many Americans cannot afford, forcing the poorest in our society to reduce or even forego the use of the Internet as a tool for commerce, education, information, exploration, and individual responsibility and opportunity.

In a society—indeed, a world—where the quality of life and an individual's opportunity for prosperity are directly related proportionately to one's access to and the acquisition of knowledge, we as a Senate must choose to close this economic digital divide rather than exacerbate it by allowing States and localities to further tax the Internet.

I call on my colleagues to join me in supporting S. 150, the Internet Tax Nondiscrimination Act, which permanently extends the Internet moratorium on access, multiple, and discriminatory taxes.

In sum, I ask my colleagues to be leaders, leaders who stand strong for individual freedom and stand strong for opportunities for all Americans.

[Congressional Record: S13791-13793]

April 26, 2004

Madam President, I rise this afternoon to urge my colleagues to support the motion for cloture to proceed to S. 150, the Internet Tax Nondiscrimination Act. This bill does have strong bipartisan support.

Let me say a few things in response to my good friend, the junior Senator from Delaware, Mr. Carper. If those who oppose this measure want to extend the moratorium, why are we having this debate tonight? Why are we going to have to have a motion for cloture on moving to proceed on the bill?

I agree that we should do no harm. Those who are for this measure want to prevent harm to consumers so that they are not loaded up with taxes from State and local governments. I will get into the details of that in my remarks.

The cost, the so-called unfunded mandate aspect of this is a very small amount in the scheme of things, $80 to $120 million, then another $40 million for the taxing of DSL. Updates in the new technologies need to be made in the definition of Internet access to make sure DSL and digital subscriber lines using telephone lines get high-speed Internet access or broadband. We need to have that changed to make sure the folks at the State and local level recognize that there has been an update and upgrade, there have been advancements in technology in the transport of the Internet, particularly broadband, but DSL lines should not be subject to taxation.

The intent of the first Internet tax moratorium was to make sure the Internet was free of taxation. The Internet is a freeway. If you want access to information, you click on. Now that transport is being taxed. Who pays? The consumer pays.

I will use an analogy. Now we have a freeway. You are going to Charlotte, NC, from Washington, DC, you get on Interstate 95 and switch over to Interstate 85. It is a freeway. Then you get off on an exit to wherever you want to get in the city of Charlotte, NC.

The advocates of taxing the Internet and those who oppose S. 150 would like to turn that freeway into the New Jersey Turnpike, a toll road.

Clearly, the consumer getting that information on the backbone of the Internet is going to have to pay for it, increasing their costs.

Companion legislation was passed by the House 8 months ago. My colleagues have heard me say on many occasions, I believe what we ought to be advocating in the Senate, in the Congress, at the Federal level, and every level of government in the United States of America, are policies that allow people to compete and succeed. That means tax policy, regulatory policies that promote freedom and opportunity for all Americans. We ought to, as leaders, be advancing ideas that help create more investment, creating, thereby, more jobs and more prosperity rather than more burdens of taxation and regulation.

Senator Wyden from Oregon and I joined together early last year with this bill. We want to make sure there is equal access to the Internet for all consumers and also protect e-commerce transactions from discriminatory taxes or multiple taxes. The Internet is one of the greatest tools invented by this country. It is a symbol and an actual tool of innovation and individual empowerment. Accordingly, I would think everyone in the Senate would want to help the Internet continue to grow and flourish as a valuable tool for commerce, for information, for education.

However, as of November 1 of last year, the Federal moratorium, which was originally enacted in 1998—and Senator Wyden was a key sponsor of that measure—expired, leaving consumers vulnerable to harmful regressive and discriminatory taxes for the first time in 6 years.

If the Senate does not act now and move to consider S. 150, it is unlikely we will get another chance in this election year. If we do not invoke cloture, the Senate will be known as a Senate that favors new taxes on the Internet; the Senate that turned a blind eye; and a Senate that limited individual opportunity while enabling harmful, regressive taxation of access to the Internet.

When Senator Wyden and I introduced this legislation over a year ago, it was consistent with the founding principles of the original moratorium that the Internet ought to remain as accessible as possible to all people in all parts of the country forever. Unfortunately, in the last year of debate, the focus has shifted away from that principle, causing unnecessary confusion and delay.

Let me be clear, this legislation is not about tax breaks for telecommunications companies. It is not about mayors and Governors. It is certainly not about the 1994 Republican revolution that has absolutely nothing to do with traditional telephone calls migrating to the Internet. Rather, our legislation has everything to do with consumers and the impact of taxation on real people and our American economy.

All of the pro-tax arguments and misleading accusations presented by the opposition are unrelated distractions aimed at confusing Senators and stalling consideration of this very important measure. In fact, the issue is not about telephone services migrating to the Internet. Rather, it is the ongoing campaign by State and local tax lobbyists to make sure telephone taxes, which average 15 to 18 percent, migrate to the Internet.

I ask my colleagues and anyone else who might be listening to think of their telephone bill. Think of the bill you receive each month with all sorts of taxes included—usually multiple local taxes, State taxes, as well as Federal taxes.

In effect, the opponents of our measure would have our monthly Internet service provider bill be loaded down with all those taxes, as on our telephone bill.

[Congressional Record: S4357]

" The best jobs in the future will go to those who are the best prepared. However, I am increasingly concerned that when it comes to high technology jobs—which pay higher wages—this country runs the risk of economically limiting many college students in our society. ... Providing equal technological opportunities for all Americans will have a positive impact on our education system, our economic competitiveness and future generations of innovators and leaders. "

DIGITAL DIVIDE

February 17, 2005

M r. President, today, with my colleagues, Senators Talent, Graham, McCain, Lott, Warner, Grassley and Thune, I rise to introduce the Minority Serving Institution Digital & Wireless Technology Opportunity Act of 2005.

This legislation will provide vital resources to address the technology gap that exists at many Minority Serving Institutions, MSIs. With this legislation together, as a country, we move one step closer to eliminating what I like to call the "economic opportunity divide" that exists between Minority Serving Institutions and non-minority institutions of higher education.

This legislation will establish a new grant program that provides up to $250 million a year to help Historically Black Colleges and Universities, Hispanic Serving Institutions, and Tribal Colleges upgrade their technology and communications infrastructure.

Since before I was elected to the Senate, my goal has always been to look for ways to improve education and empower all of our young people—regardless of their race, ethnicity, religion or economic background—to compete and succeed in life.

With over 200 Hispanic Serving Institutions; over 100 Historically Black Colleges and Universities and 34 tribal colleges throughout our country, it is clear that Minority Serving Institutions provide a valuable service to the educational strength and future growth of our Nation.

These institutions must have the technology capabilities and infrastructure available to their students and faculty to successfully compete and succeed in today's workforce.

Our goal with this legislation is clear—by increasing access to technology and addressing the technological disparities that exist at Minority Serving Institutions we will provide our young people with important tools for success, both in the classroom and in the workforce.

This nation's economic stability and growth are increasingly dependent on a growing portion of the workforce possessing technological skills.

African Americans, Hispanics and Native Americans constitute one-quarter of the total U.S. workforce. Approximately, one-third of all students of color in this nation are educated at Minority Serving Institutions. It is estimated that in 10 years minorities will comprise nearly 40 percent of all college-age Americans.

Yet, members of these minorities represent only 7 percent of the U.S. computer and information science workforce; 6 percent of the engineering workforce; and less than 2 percent of the computer science faculty.

At the same time, we know that 60 percent of all jobs require information technology skills and these jobs pay significantly higher salaries than jobs of a non-technical nature.

I am proud to say Virginia is home to five Historically Black Colleges & Universities—Norfolk State University, St. Paul's College, Virginia Union University, Hampton University and Virginia State University.

Mr. President, we must ensure that the students attending these minority institutions are competing on a level playing field when it comes to technology skills and development.

We must tap the talent and potential of these students to ensure that America's workforce is prepared to lead the world.

The legislation allows eligible institutions the opportunity through grants, contracts or cooperative agreements to acquire equipment, instrumentation, networking capability, hardware and software, digital network technology and wireless technology/infrastructure—such as wireless fidelity or WiFi—to develop and provide educational services.

Additionally, the grants can be used for equipment upgrades, technology training and hardware/software acquisition. A Minority Serving Institution also can use the funds to offer its students universal access to campus networks, dramatically increase their connectivity rates, or make necessary infrastructure improvements.

The best jobs in the future will go to those who are the best prepared. However, I am increasingly concerned that when it comes to high technology jobs—which pay higher wages—this country runs the risk of economically limiting many college students in our society. It is important for all Americans that we close this opportunity gap.

Providing equal technological opportunities for all Americans will have a positive impact on our education system, our economic competitiveness and future generations of innovators and leaders.

I encourage all of my colleagues to support this legislation. This exact legislation passed the Senate last year 97-0.

Mr. President, I want to thank my colleagues for joining me today in cosponsoring this legislation and I look forward to working with fellow Senators to push this important measure across the goal-line so that many more college students are provided access to better technology and education, and most importantly, even greater opportunities in life.

[Congressional Record: S1652-1653]

" There is a debate currently underway in our country over which types of tax cuts are the answer to providing immediate economic growth. In my judgment, we must focus on individual tax cuts that will immediately lift consumer confidence and result in greater consumer spending—the idea that we need to increase corporate savings and investment necessities, that those companies have revenues in the first place, revenues that come from consumer spending. "

Economy, Consumer Spending, and Education Tax Credit

October 1, 2001

Mr. President, I rise to share with my colleagues my concern about our economy, the loss of jobs, and the economic stimulus package being considered by Members of the House, the Senate, and the White House. Mr. Thomas, the Senator from Wyoming, mentioned some of the economic stimulus package. In my view, an education opportunity tax credit should be included in any economic stimulus package put together in the coming weeks.

We know our economy is in serious trouble. The economy grew just 0.2 of 1 percent in the second quarter of this year, compared to 4.1-percent average growth in the year 2000. The most important thing we can do at this point is increase consumer spending, especially on durable goods. Orders for durable goods dropped in August, as reported by the Commerce Department, all of which was due to the technology and transportation sectors. We have addressed the transportation industry partially, with the airline industry stabilization bill, but the technology sector still remains unaddressed.

Consumer confidence is dropping like a stone. The University of Michigan Consumer Sentiment Index released last week, September 28, indicated that consumer confidence dropped 21 percent. Although the correlation between consumer confidence and spending is not strong in the short term, it is strong in the mid-to-long term. The No. 1 reason for this precipitous drop in consumer confidence is because of where consumers thought they would be in their own lives 6 months out. One financial market analyst was recently quoted in the *Washington Post* as saying that the size of this decline in consumer confidence will translate into reduced spending in the next 6 months. That confidence decline is not over. Consumers, clearly, are on a very cautious mindset. That is why we must take measures to improve consumer confidence and spending again.

There is a debate currently underway in our country over which types of tax cuts are the answer to providing immediate economic growth. In my judgment, we must focus on individual tax cuts that will immediately lift consumer confidence and result in greater consumer spending—the idea that we need to increase corporate savings and investment necessities, that those companies have revenues in the first place, revenues that come from consumer spending.

Instead, what is needed, as the *Wall Street Journal* editorialized today, is "temporary, not permanent tax breaks—and preferably for consumers, not business."

The Wall Street Journal article was very clear as to the ineffectiveness of corporate tax cuts in order to spur the economy, citing Gregory Mankiw, an economist at Harvard, who favors permanently abolishing the corporate income tax, but states that doing so now would not result in immediate investment. He is quoted as saying:

"The problem now is there's a lot of uncertainty, which is inducing people to wait, which depresses aggregate demand, which in turn exacerbates the economic slowdown."

The Wall Street Journal further opines that:

"… stimulating spending and making members feel secure would be more effective than reducing corporate tax rates as a way to boost economic growth."

In fact, we all know our economy, this free market, is all about the consumer. If consumers do not buy, companies will not have revenue. If companies do not have revenue, they will not be able to invest, nor will companies need employees to be in those jobs to produce.

If they do not invest, if they are not creating jobs, our economy will not grow out of this economic sluggishness.

The technology sector, which was once the leading force behind economic growth and productivity, is now the most significant detractor, getting hit the hardest by the contractions in spending and investment. There has been a 19-percent drop in technology spending, including a 45-percent drop in personal computer orders and a 14.5-percent drop in software and equipment spending.

Other sources of capital and growth have dried up as well. Banks continue to limit their exposure to the high-technology sector and tighten lending standards, cutting off resources at a time when money is already scarce. Venture capital has all but disappeared from this sector. First-round venture capital funding has already fallen $1.84 billion, down 87 percent from the previous year during the second quarter of 2001.

This has all led to widespread layoffs within the tech sector over this past year. Job cuts in the high-tech industries of telecommunications, computers and electronics—those job cuts are up 13 times over what they were last year.

Through the end of August, high tech accounted for nearly 40 percent of the 1.1 million job cuts so far in 2001.

Just to put that in perspective, that is 4 times more, 4 times greater than the entire post-attack airline industry layoffs—over 400,000 jobs lost in the tech sector versus, obviously, a great concern over 100,000 jobs lost in the airline industry sector. The total tech job sector cuts in August alone exceeded all of the cuts for the year 2000.

This technology sluggishness is clearly harmful for our future. Technological advancements are how America and our economy will compete and succeed internationally, and technological sector growth and rapid advances in productivity have been the base of our economic growth in the past and will be a vital key to our competitiveness in the future. As we look at technology in the future, whether it is computers, whether it is clean coal technology, whether it is fuel cell technology, these are important for future competitiveness, our quality of life, and good jobs in the future.

The lifeline to our economy, consumer spending, has been seriously dampened by the terrorist attacks which occurred on September 11, 2001. That is why I would like to bring the attention of my colleagues back to a bill I introduced in March of this year, the Educational Opportunity Tax Credit of 2001. This proposal will provide a $1,000-per-child computer purchase tax credit which families can also use, not just to buy computers but printers, monitors, educational software, or Internet access. However, this tax credit would not apply to tuition at a private school. This would provide the exact type of boost both consumer spending on durable goods and the technology sector need. Maybe we could limit this tax credit to 1 or 2 years. Even with that limitation I would estimate it would provide upwards of $20 billion in new consumer spending.

Think of parents who have a child in school. If they could buy their son or daughter a computer or some peripherals, a printer, they would say: Gosh, if I do it this year or next year, I will get a tax break for it. That will induce that spending.

It clearly would induce computer and technology spending, especially if it is available for 2 years, thus propelling the technology sector while also improving educational opportunities for students. The fact is, experience shows that even a small, temporary reduction in taxes can bring about huge increases in computer sales.

In South Carolina, they had a sales tax holiday on computers for just 3 days. CPU sales increased more than tenfold; 1,060 percent in those 3 days.

In the Commonwealth of Pennsylvania they eliminated the sales tax on computers for 1 week. CPU sales increased six fold; 615 percent in that time.

My Educational Opportunity Tax Credit would not just impact computer sales but also software makers, Internet access providers, printer, monitor and scanner manufacturers as well.

In South Carolina they realized a 664-percent and 700-percent increase in monitor and printer sales, respectively, with only a 5-percent tax break. We know that consumer spending accounts for two-thirds of all economic activity, which is largely flat and has been flat this summer and weakening in the last report in our economy.

The Education Opportunity Tax Credit represents the right solution for our economy. No. 1, it increases consumer spending on computers and related technology. No. 2, it injects $20 billion into the weakest and one of the very important links in our economy. No. 3, it provides previously out-of-reach education and technology opportunities for families.

As I said before, I am willing to work with my colleagues in addressing the best way to implement this proposal. We can shorten the applicable timeframe from the original bill. We can look at a different credit level to make sure we get the maximum economic impact for minimum fiscal impact to the Treasury. But I am convinced that combining consumer-oriented tax cuts with appreciation of what is really going on in the technology sector can improve consumer confidence, accelerate consumer spending, and provide the technology sector the revenues they need to reinvest and return our economy to strong growth and also provide more good paying jobs for the people of America.

[Congressional Record: S9942-9943]

“ Closing the digital divide is important. The education opportunity tax credit provides the financial resources to achieve this goal by making the tax credit fully refundable so that lower income families who owe the Government less money than the maximum available tax credit … or if they have no tax liability at all, would get the full credit. Everyone would be able to take full advantage of this opportunity. ”

EDUCATION OPPORTUNITY TAX CREDIT

March 13, 2001

M r. President, I rise today in support of the education opportunity tax credit on behalf of myself as well as Senators Warner, Craig, and Allard. This is a measure that was introduced last Thursday, March 8.

What the education opportunity tax credit would do is increase the amount and the quality of available academic services and technology-related resources for parents and for students.

This measure does several very good things. No. 1, it increases education spending with greater parental involvement. No. 2, it is a tax cut for families. And, No. 3, it brings forth more funds available for technology and specialized tutoring-type teaching.

I know the Presiding Officer and other Members of the Senate recognize how important education is for our children and for the future of our

Nation. It is essential for our children's futures because the best jobs will go to those who are the best prepared. The education opportunity tax credit helps in that regard.

In education, good quality classrooms and good teachers, able to impart knowledge to our children, are important. Academic standards and account-ability and the measurement of those high academic standards in the basics of English, math, science, social studies, and economics are all important, but also as important as teachers and administrators in the education of our children are the parents; and parents need to be empowered. Their involve-ment is key for the academic success of their children.

Indeed, parents know their children's names. They know the specific needs of their children much more than any bureaucracy in Washington, DC.

Finally, children need to have computer skills to be able to compete and succeed in the future. Computers and wiring in schools and access to the Internet in schools and in libraries is a good idea and is very important. Community centers are important.

Last week, the Republican Senate High-Tech Task Force visited an Intel clubhouse. It is working in conjunction with the Boys and Girls Club here in Washington, DC. There are many good ideas in these community centers, but we need to make sure there are computers and software programs and educational programs at home because homework is done at home and on weekends.

This is what the education opportunity tax credit does. It provides fami-lies with a $1,000-per-child education opportunity tax credit. It is capped at $1,000 per year per child, and capped at $2,000 per year per family if they have more than one child. It defrays the cost of education-related expenses for computers and computer-related accessories and technology. Educational software, Internet access, and tutoring services could be expenditures that would thereby get the tax credit. It does not apply to private school tuition. And as introduced, it is refundable.

This is a family-oriented education tax incentive that will have a very real impact on the ability of parents to better afford education-related services and technology resources.

This is the financial situation of a family with an income of $38,900. That is the median family income in the United States.

After a family pays all the money in taxes to the Federal Government, the State Government, the local government, and after they pay for their housing, their clothing, their food, their medical care, and their transportation—these are all absolutely essential for the survival of a family—the real disposable income gets down to about $2,100.

Now, educational expenses normally are going to be school supplies and a variety of other items that are important. But you realize, with that amount of money, if you bought a computer, purchased a used printer, software, and Internet access, that totals over $2,400. So the amount that would be added to credit card debt would be $241 a year.

The reality is, once you pay your taxes to all levels of government, once you pay for food and clothing and housing and putting gas in the car, and a car payment, and all the rest, the average family has about $180 left a month for everything else. And the average cost of a computer is going to be about 70 percent of that.

You can have the statistics, but real people in the real world, folks such as Jim and June Meadows, support this proposal because it would help them afford specialized software for their daughter Morgan, who has dyslexia, without sacrificing the education needs of their other daughter, Meghan, who is age 10.

You do not have to go outside the beltway to find these working folks. In fact, right here in the Capitol you will find people who are working who recognize the value of this. In fact, Milton Salvadore, who I ran into in the Senate restaurant a few weeks ago, is such a working family man—he works, his wife works, and they have young children—I asked him: Do you all have a computer for your young school-aged children?

He said: "No. No."

I said: "Why not?"

He said: "Look, we have all these bills, and so forth. My wife and I are working hard, but we do not have enough money for that. We do not want to go into debt to go get a computer and Internet access for our children."

He said it would help him and his hard-working wife afford a computer for his family, if this education opportunity tax credit were in effect.

The tax impact on the average family of three with an adjusted gross income of approximately $39,000 a year, if they took the full $1,000 tax credit for their children's education expenses, that would save nearly 34 percent on their yearly Federal tax bill. A family of four with an income of $39,000 taking the full $2,000-per-family tax credit would realize a savings of 95 percent on their taxes owed for the year.

If we are going to seriously address the digital divide—and the digital divide is a divide in opportunities—we must act to provide families and children with the financial means to take advantage of education opportunities. Closing the digital divide is important. The education opportunity tax credit provides the financial resources to achieve this goal by making the tax credit fully refundable so that lower income families who owe the Government less money than the maximum available tax credit—say they owe $700—or if they have no tax liability at all, would get the full credit. Everyone would be able to take full advantage of this opportunity.

The digital divide is a function of many factors, including geography and educational levels of parents. Hence, the most salient and determinative factor is family income. According to numbers released in October of 2000 by the U.S. Department of Commerce—these figures are borne out by studies by Virginia Commonwealth University—we find that of the 92 percent of people who are computer owners, 29 percent have Internet access. So these figures do match in that regard with Virginia. If we look at households with less than $15,000 in annual income, 12.7 percent of them have Internet access, which is pretty much equal to computer ownership. Families falling within the $15,000 to $24,000 per year range have a 21-percent rate of Internet access. Families with incomes of $75,000 per year or more have about a 77-percent Internet access rate.

These numbers show how this bill will help all people, but that the main value will be to those of middle income and lower middle income who will be able to purchase computers, Internet access, and educational computer software for their children. This is more than just a purely personalized education tax and parental involvement technology issue. This is about—the digital divide and making sure people are getting a good education and access to technology so they are literate and capable. It is vital to the future of the United States in a global economy. It is important for our domestic economy, and it is obviously important for individual families.

In maintaining our economic growth, the Department of Commerce estimates that information technology industries accounted for 30 percent of the country's total real economic growth between 1995 and 1999. Between just 1997 and 1999, there were over 1.2 million new jobs. The average wage of technology jobs in the Nation was $58,000 compared to $32,000 in the overall economy.

What we need to understand is, without a continued influx of qualified, competent workers, the growth in the technology industries will stall and Americans, if not properly educated, will not be able to seize the opportunities. Whether it is in the Silicon Valley of California, the silicon Dominion of Virginia, or whether it is in Idaho, Pennsylvania, Florida, Iowa, or anywhere else, it is important that our youngsters are getting a solid education.

The number of U.S. college graduates with high-tech degrees in the country is declining. Since 1990, the number of high-tech degrees has dropped by 2 percent. Undergraduate degrees in math have declined by 21 percent, computer science degrees have declined by 37 percent, and electrical engineering degrees by 45 percent. Although, this wasn't the trend we saw in Virginia in the 1990s. Actually, there was a big increase of jobs and degrees—Virginia having the third fastest growth in technology jobs—however there was the same income differential between technology-related jobs and other forms of employment. The studies from Virginia showed that the average technology job paid $66,000 a year versus $31,000 in the overall economy.

As a country, unless we better prepare all students, they will not be able to meet the high-tech job demand; the number of innovations and new technology developments will decline, and businesses and jobs will move offshore.

I say to my colleagues in the Senate, it is time for us to act to make sure we keep these well-paying jobs, these high-tech jobs, in America for Americans.

There is broad-based support by Virginia voters for the education opportunity tax credit. This is not a conservative versus liberal, or Democrat versus Republican, or men versus women type issue; it is a commonsense, good for families, education spending and tax cut issue.

What we found in Virginia with this idea—and it did get pretty well debated in the recent campaign—is that—and this was from polling—61 percent of liberals liked the idea; 69 percent of conservatives liked it, and moderates actually liked it the best, 71 percent. Men liked it at over 70 percent. It was supported by nearly 70 percent of women. It didn't matter someone's race, where they lived, ideology or political persuasion, or if they were not involved in any organized political party. It was very strongly supported by everyone in Virginia.

The people of Virginia recognize that it helps them with their own children. In fact, at the Flying J truck stop in Caroline County, I was going in to pay my bill, and the woman who was there taking my credit card said: "I like your education tax credit."

I said: "That's great, ma'am. I am glad you know what is going on with this measure. Do you like it?"

She said: "I am a tutor in Caroline County schools in mathematics."

It is a county with many people who cannot afford a tutor, and she saw that those students who needed help in math and their families could better afford her or other tutoring services so they could get up to speed in mathematics with the support of this tax credit. This is an idea that is appreciated by people in Virginia. As we work to make sure our fellow Senators know about this idea, they will realize it is something on which we will need to have to take action very soon, to make sure our students have the highest quality and most appropriate education possible.

We need to trust parents to be involved in their schools. They know their children's needs. They know their specific areas that will be of interest and what will best benefit them. Through this substantial tax benefit, all families will have access to a full spectrum of available education opportunities and related technologies.

I hope my colleagues will look into this matter. The Education Opportunity Tax Credit Act will provide families with choice and opportunity. I look forward to working with my colleagues, Senator Warner of Virginia, Senator Craig of Idaho, and Senator Allard of Colorado, as well as other Members, in making sure that we ensure the passage of the education opportunity tax credit to empower parents, to increase education spending, and also to reduce taxes while providing more technology capabilities to the children of America.

[Congressional Record: S2171-2172]

" As the global economy brings in new opportunities and greater prosperity, all families will need ready access to the technical and technological skills and tools necessary for students to succeed in a classroom and also in the digital economy. "

EDUCATION, PARENTS
AND TECHNOLOGY

May 7, 2001

M r. President, having listened to the impassioned words of the
Senator from Massachusetts, Mr. Kennedy, and knowing the
great leadership that he and Senator Jeffords, chairman of the HELP
Committee, have provided on education, it is very good for the American
people to recognize how important education is to those of us at the Federal
level. Education is not just a Federal responsibility; it is primarily a State and
local responsibility.

The actions that have been taken so far and will be taken in the days to
come will result in the Federal Government being there to be of help and
assistance to local schools, to parents, and, most importantly, to students in
getting a good education. Indeed, all of us can agree that ensuring that our
children receive the best possible education is one of the most important
responsibilities to the people in our States and all across America.

Quality education, why do we care about it? Because a quality education
is absolutely necessary for our children and all children across this country to

be able to compete, succeed, and lead a fulfilling life. It is key for their future success, personally and professionally. It allows them, with a good education, economic freedom and financial security. A good education allows someone greater career opportunities and choices and mobility. It also allows them to provide for themselves financially as well as for their family. Education also is very important to society and for our American civilization to compete and succeed internationally.

I was made chair of the Senate Republican high-tech task force. One of our key policy agenda items is in promoting education and technology. I quote from our policy agenda:

"Without a workforce fully capable in math, science and computing skills, our competitiveness is at risk. Without a consumer base able to utilize the latest technological advances, our economic growth may wane. The task force believes that a top priority in education should be the development of policies that encourage the use of technology."

I speak as a father. I speak with my previous experience as Governor and also as a candidate with certain promises I made to the people of Virginia, should I be elected, in the area of education. We talked about the need for more teachers, allowing the localities to determine what those needs would be as far as funding for teachers, whether they use increased salaries for existing teachers, pay stipends for math and science teachers; whether it is hiring more teachers; that is important to reduce class size so children in the early grades get more individualized attention. There is action, activity so far on this measure and will be in the days to come to improve it.

The early reading initiative, which we started in Virginia, is part of the package. It is very important to make sure youngsters at the earliest grades—kindergarten, first and second—are reading at speed. Of all the academic subjects, nothing is more important than reading. We have testing in Virginia, as do many other States. Testing and standards are very important for identification of children who need additional help as well as giving parents a school performance report card.

I agree with the outstanding amendments Senator Jeffords put forth last week to make sure the Federal requirement of testing in a couple subjects would not become an unfunded mandate. What we ought to do is empower and help local schools, certainly not add unfunded mandates. Senator Jeffords' leadership in that regard was essential, and, fortunately, it passed overwhelmingly.

Another good thing about this measure so far is that it seems the Federal Government is trusting localities and States with greater flexibility to identify what their specific needs are in that particular school district.

That is important.

Now, in addition to all of this, the President has gotten involved, so obviously it has been a priority. The House and Senate have been involved, and we have made it a priority.

As important as our local school boards and State governments and the Federal Government are, parents are important. For a good student, you will find that you need good teachers, yes, and they need to be in a good environment. But also key is good parents.

I want to take this opportunity to focus on increasing access to technology for those students in grades kindergarten through 12th grade.

We all understand, and I think the Presiding Officer today sure understands, how technology has fueled the unprecedented growth and transformed the way Americans conduct business and communicate with one another. As the global economy brings in new opportunities and greater prosperity, all families will need ready access to the technical and technological skills and tools necessary for students to succeed in a classroom and also in the digital economy.

Together schools, communities, and government have worked to bring computers to the classrooms and integrate technology into daily classroom curriculums. Classroom connectivity has soared from 14 percent in 1996 to 63 percent in 1999. When I was Governor, we finally were able to get the Goals 2000 money and put it into Network Virginia, to connect all our colleges, community colleges, and schools. So that has been going on across the country.

The Elementary and Secondary Education Act provides a separate funding stream for teacher technology training, which is important. There are tax incentives for companies to donate computers to schools. That is going on in Virginia and across the U.S. However, it is not enough that there be a computer present in the classroom or in a community center. I think it is great what Intel is doing with the Girls and Boys Clubs with their computer club houses. That is really good. But I also would like to see people have computers at home. Only through consistent access to technology can students develop the necessary technical skills to succeed and compete in the future marketplace and economy. Children must have access to the Internet at home so they can better complete after school homework. If you want the children to be able to have access to information or to do word processing, all that ought to be done on a computer at home, and they should not have to go to the school or a library or a community center.

The homework assignments are done after school and on weekends, and I think also by having the children working on computers at home, that increases their programming and technological skills. It also allows them to discover additional academic opportunities. There are some great educational software programs in geography, history, math, science, and the language arts, which all go at the pace of the student who is on the computer. E-books are coming around and that is another way of having children get interested in reading in a more easy way.

All of this, again, is gathered at the pace of the students. Studies have shown that the presence of a computer in the home has a positive impact on a student's level of academic achievement and performance in the school. For example, a study using NAEP data found that eighth graders who use computers frequently at home demonstrated higher levels of academic achievement than those who do not. Parents in those situations became more involved with the daily assignments, and it also increases their communication with teachers through the use of e-mail.

There was a study in a New York project where children actually were given laptops, personal computers—they weren't just in the classroom and the library—and they were allowed to bring the personal computers home. The training was provided in this project in New York. Not only did it increase academic performance, but it had long-term benefits. The results were that the participants were more likely to stay in school, graduate, and go on to college.

Earlier this year, with the support of my colleagues, Senators Warner, Allard, Hutchinson, Craig, and Hutchison, I introduced the Education Opportunity Tax Credit Act, which would provide financial relief for the purchase of technology and tutorial services for K-12 educational purposes. My proposal would provide a $1,000 tax credit per year, up to $2,000 per family, for the cost of their children's education-related expenses—specifically computer peripherals and computer-related technology, educational software, Internet access, and tutoring services. However, the tax credit would not apply toward the cost of private school tuition.

This proposal would significantly help defray the cost of educational expenses by empowering families financially and thereby increasing educational spending, which would mostly be on technology. Even more important, the education opportunity tax credit would improve the quality of educational experiences for students by allowing families to provide their children with access to a far greater range of educational opportunities suited to their individual needs. It would encourage parental involvement in their children's education. Indeed, parents are the ones who know their children's needs, know their names, and know their specific problem areas, and we need to empower parents. Furthermore, this idea of providing this tax relief for the purchase of educational technology would also help bridge the digital divide. It is very important that everyone has an equal opportunity—whether it is tax policies, regulatory policies, or educational and technological policies—so that everyone can seize the opportunities in this digital age and this information technology economy.

Mr. President, the amendment I am introducing today would provide for a sense of the Senate in affirming how important it is that we increase opportunities for home access to technology for school-age children. While I am unable to offer the education opportunity tax credit to S. 1 because tax provisions cannot generally be added to a program authorization bill, by voting to support this sense-of-the-Senate amendment, we will be setting the foundation for future progress on this important matter.

Generally, I believe we are on the right track, for the most part, on educational reform at the Federal level with this bill. There is more trust and decision making at the State and local levels. There are more funds and will be more funds for teachers, early reading initiatives, and protecting against unfunded mandates. This is due in no small part to Senators Jeffords and Gregg and other Members and the White House and leadership from both sides of the aisle.

Remember how we get a good student: You need good schools and parents.

We need to not only thank the leaders in the Senate for the good work they are doing but also make sure that we don't forget the parents. We need to empower parents to provide these technological educational schools for their children so their children have the same opportunities as all children, and also make sure that our country can compete and succeed. As we move forward on educational reform, I am confident that we will also be able to increase access to education-related technology for all children in their homes and pass the education opportunity tax credit into law.

I believe if we work on both sides of the aisle, we would understand that children need to have computers at home, access to the Internet, and the world of information that comes from having an individualized Library of Congress right there at home for our children.

[Congressional Record: S4437-4439]

> " It is for the parents, teachers, and community, not Washington, to know what is best for students. We want to provide students with a safe learning environment, but we do not need any illogical interference from the Federal Government. ... "

EDUCATION AND LOCAL CONTROL

June 14, 2001

Mr. President, I rise in support of the Sessions amendment which would properly return the ability to the local schools and principals to establish and implement uniform discipline policies applicable to all children in our States and school districts.

I have been listening to a lot of comments back and forth. One of the reasons this issue comes back year after year after year is that it is an issue in local schools year after year after year and it becomes an issue in campaigns.

The issue is not whether or not we support IDEA or support education and helping those with disabilities. We clearly all agree with that. The issue is whether or not we are going to have a uniform standard of conduct applicable to all students within a public school system. That is the issue.

I was involved in this issue from the first month I came in as Governor of Virginia in 1994 where we had these problems with this Federal law. We took the Department of Education to court in *Commonwealth of Virginia v. Riley*. We went to the appellate court and prevailed. Then in 1997 our victory for maintaining order and discipline in our schools was taken away by the action of the House and the Senate.

I can promise the Senator from Iowa, the Senator from Massachusetts, and the Senator from Alabama that discipline or expulsion is not taken lightly in Alabama or Virginia—or I can't imagine in any school. To accuse our educators, our States, our school boards of wanting to unfairly discriminate against students with disabilities and shirking their responsibility by unfairly expelling them is unfounded and wrong.

It is not a question of a kid smoking a cigarette in the parking lot. The issues are students who set up cocaine rings, sell explosives that blow off a child's hand, or bloody another student with brass knuckles. If a child has an epileptic fit and breaks a teacher's nose, that is usually a mitigating factor so a child will not be expelled.

Here are actual cases in Fairfax County, not too far from here, in public schools. A group of students brought in a loaded 357 magnum handgun. It was recovered in the school building. The non-special-education students were expelled. One student, however, was identified as learning disabled due to the student's weakness in written language skills. The team reviewed the evaluations and found there was no causal relationship between the student's writing disability and the student's involvement in the weapons violation. The student was not expelled. That student later bragged to teachers and students at the school that he could not be expelled.

In another recent case in Fairfax High School, a student was part of a gang that was involved in a mob assault on another student. One student involved in the melee used a meat hook as a weapon. Three of the gang members were expelled; the other two who were special ed students were not expelled and are still in the school.

These are the real situations where there is not an equal or fair administration of standards of conduct in the schools. I think we all care about good school conduct. We want small class sizes, good academics, good assessments, empowerment of parents, and all the rest. What also is important is a conducive learning environment.

We need to trust in and take care to allow the responsibilities for maintaining order and discipline in schools to be where they properly belong and not have a Federal law that really justifies a double standard on discipline for disabled and non disabled students, despite our shared efforts to ensure equal treatment and inclusion into a mainstream system.

The Sessions amendment would return authority for all students back to the States and local schools where it belongs. It is for the parents, teachers, and community, not Washington, to know what is best for students. We want to provide students with a safe learning environment, but we do not need any illogical interference from the Federal Government. ...

Mr. President, in response to some of the remarks by the Senator from Massachusetts, let me say this is not an issue about trying to deprive those students with disabilities of an education. This is an issue of standards of conduct. Oh, sure, the Federal Government does put some money into IDEA, but most of it does come from the taxpayers of the Commonwealth of Massachusetts, the Commonwealth of Virginia, and the State of Alabama. That is the whole issue of the Harkin-Hagel amendment in the first place. It has been an unfunded mandate.

To cite the comments and cast aspersions on my remarks, which were taken from a court decision—these individuals from Richmond City public schools, Fairfax County public schools, were under oath. Just because a General Accounting Office report doesn't refer to these situations doesn't mean they did not occur. Those individuals presented themselves before a court and swore under oath what happened. There are school records of it. They were subject to cross-examination.

For the Senator from Massachusetts to say these are just concocted, falsified stories, unfortunately is not an accurate statement. These are incidents that occur time after time.

The Senator from Alabama and I are not saying that disabled students cause trouble all the time. But it does happen, from students who are disabled and students who have no disabilities—they cause problems in schools. We think the standards of conduct should be fair and equal in their treatment, with proper due process and equal protection. That is what the issue is, and no amount of unfair aspersions, raised voices, and histrionics can avoid the facts of what we are trying to do, to preserve local autonomy and safe schools as well as equal and fair treatment.

[Congressional Record: S6244-6247]

" Hard-working Americans, facing such a harrowing situation, ought to have a response to help them get through the early stages of the economy recovery until jobs become more readily available and workers can provide for their families. The 13 weeks of extended benefits provides the temporary financial assistance for displaced workers to get back on their feet and successfully get a new job. "

JOB CREATION

March 13, 2002

Madam President, it is with great relief that I rise today in commendation for approval of the "Job Creation and Worker Assistance Act of 2002," which I believe represents a job security, job creation and balanced response by the Federal Government to the economic challenges faced by families and businesses. With the signing of this Act into law, on March 9, 2002, by the President, Americans finally received the economic stimulus relief that should have been passed many months ago.

During the past months, all Americans have been deluged with grim news of recessions, plummeting consumer confidence and rising unemployment. Last March, which is widely believed to be the beginning of the current recession, unemployment totaled 6.2 million, or 4.3 percent. Just under a year later, February unemployment rate equaled 5.5 percent, a number representative of the 1.4 million jobs lost since March of last year.

These numbers represent much more than just mere statistics, the 5.5 percent represents 7.9 million people who are without a job, a steady paycheck and the security of knowing that bills will be paid and food will be on the table. Even more worrisome for many families is that they have begun to exhaust their State unemployment benefits: in January 2002 alone, 373,000 displaced workers ran out of the financial support they need to simply survive as they look for a job.

This is why ending the obstruction by passage of the Job Creation and Worker Assistance Act of 2002 is so important. This bill not only includes targeted tax incentives that will increase capital investment and spending, ensuring that the weak recovery underway will not be derailed, but it provides the economic security the families of displaced workers so desperately need to get by until new jobs can be found.

I would like to take this opportunity to talk briefly about two provisions that I am particularly pleased are included in the economic stimulus package.

First, this recession is notable for the sharp plummet in the level of capital investment in new equipment and technologies by companies, coupled with a decrease in consumer demand. Until such capital expenditures increase, our economy will not fully recover from the recession.

Accelerated depreciation is a top priority of Virginia's and America's technology industry. It will spur capital expenditures for new advanced equipment and technology. This incentive will create and save more jobs for working men and women involved in producing, creating, fabricating and transporting such capital equipment from computers and construction equipment to airplanes and locomotives.

By providing for a 30-percent bonus depreciation rate over a 3-year period, the economic stimulus package will encourage enterprising businesses and people to invest and grow, promoting capital expenditures that would not have occurred but for the passage of this act, eventually increasing job growth and consumer spending.

Second, the bill includes a provision, similar to legislation I introduced in September 2001, which provides displaced workers with an additional 13 weeks of unemployment benefits after they have exhausted their State-provided unemployment benefits.

Recently, we have received good news on the economy and the prospects of its recovery from the recession. February was the first month in which jobs were added since July 2001, and the unemployment rate is finally beginning to inch down from its high of 5.8 percent in December 2001.

Yet, even with the good news, Chairman Greenspan is still maintaining his earlier forecast of relatively weak economic growth in 2002 of between 2.5 percent and 3 percent. It will take time for the economy to fully recover and to create the jobs that will get workers back on the payrolls. News of eventual recovery is of little relief for the 1.4 million workers who have exhausted their unemployment benefits since September 2001.

Without the immediate financial life-line that the additional 13 weeks of benefits provides, these families, at the minimum, risk ruining their credit ratings and, in the worst-case scenario, could lose their home or car.

Hard-working Americans, facing such a harrowing situation, ought to have a response to help them get through the early stages of the economy recovery until jobs become more readily available and workers can provide for their families. The 13 weeks of extended benefits provides the temporary financial assistance for displaced workers to get back on their feet and successfully get a new job.

In sum, the Job Creation and Worker Assistance Act of 2002 is the appropriate combination of immediate financial relief and security to American families and tax incentives for businesses to make the capital investments necessary for economic growth and job creation. I am confident that the new opportunities made available with the passage of this act will go a long way toward ensuring a more secure future for American working men, women and families.

[Congressional Record: S1855]

"[W]e want to make sure every American, regardless of their race, their gender, their ethnicity, or their religious beliefs, has the opportunity to compete and succeed. That means our tax policies have to be conducive to investment. Regulations need to be based on sound science, not political science."

JOB CREATION AND ECONOMIC REGULATION

November 17, 2003

Mr. President, I thank my colleagues for joining with us in this debate on the most important issue we have facing us in the Senate and in our country. That is: How can we work to make sure we have the best policies for more investment and more job creation?

The reality is, right now things are getting better. They need to get better, though, than they are currently. Nevertheless, the facts are clear. Job growth is up by 126,000 in October. When my colleagues talk about the last 20 years, last month we had an annual growth rate of 7.2 percent.

That is the best in 20 years.

The Republicans' point of view, I would say to my colleagues, is that we want to make sure every American, regardless of their race, their gender, their ethnicity, or their religious beliefs, has the opportunity to compete and succeed. That means our tax policies have to be conducive to investment. Regulations need to be based on sound science, not political science.

We also need to make sure the people of our country, in our States, have the capabilities and the knowledge to get the good jobs in the future. We also need to have security. When we see people in communities worried about crime or worried about terrorism, those are adverse impacts, on confidence and investment and therefore job creation. We have seen the adverse impacts of 9/11, particularly in the travel and tourism industry.

I know as Governor of the Commonwealth of Virginia what matters to businesses when they are looking to invest. They look at what is the cost of doing business, what is the tax rate, what is the cost of workers compensation. Ours are low in Virginia because we keep lawyers out of workers compensation. We get the money to the person who is injured so he or she can get back to work. Unemployment insurance taxes matter. The fact that we have a right to work law, which gives individuals the right, if they so desire, not to join a union as a condition of work, that helps attract business. Health insurance matters as well.

In a variety of areas, we have found Virginia ended up with much more job growth, more investment. It was called the Silicon Dominion because of the investment, because of having taxes competitively low, prompt permitting, reasonable regulations, and also investment in security and also in the capabilities of our students for high academic standards.

The Democrats talk about all of these Presidents. Interesting. Richard Nixon was elected after President Johnson. If one wants to call Jimmy Carter their second best President, with the malaise and the high interest rates, the high unemployment, and the high inflation. People put in Ronald Reagan to help revive this economy and make us stronger as well as, of course, keep our peace through strength.

I find it interesting my good friend from Iowa talks about, oh, the Republicans somehow want to imperil Social Security and gets off on these tangents on privatization. Of course the Democrats care about Social Security because in 1993 they not only taxed all families and all small businesses and every taxpayer, they even taxed Social Security benefits. When given the opportunity most recently on a measure introduced by Senator Bunning of the Commonwealth of Kentucky, virtually every Democrat voted against that effort to repeal the tax on Social Security benefits.

The fact is, we are making good progress. We need to keep moving forward. We have ideas, as Republicans, in a variety of ways that we can make sure the American economy can compete internationally, can help create more jobs and greater opportunity. Indeed, we want to make health care costs more affordable and predictable, reduce the burden of lawsuits on our economy, whether it is asbestos reform or class action reform, make sure we have an affordable, reliable energy supply, streamline regulations, open new markets for American products, and also make sure there is confidence in investment in this country by making sure the tax reductions are permanent.

I will close with the words of Mr. Jefferson who said that the Government should restrain men from injuring one another but otherwise leave them free to regulate their own pursuits of industry and improvement and shall not take from the mouths of labor the bread they have earned.

That remains the sum of good government today.

[Congressional Record: S14953]

"Simply put, we are entirely too dependent on foreign oil and we must expand our domestic production. … Diversification of energy supplies is basic to our comprehensive national energy policy. We should encourage new, cooperative trade arrangements and new resources in willing prospects throughout the world."

ENERGY, FOREIGN OIL
AND DOMESTIC
PRODUCTION

April 11, 2002

M r. President, I rise today to discuss the much needed energy security legislation that is before the Senate.

This week, at the very moment we debate this very important landmark legislation, we are seeing a confluence of factors in our energy supply and demand that amounts to what one might call the "perfect storm."

There have been few other times in the history of our nation where we have seen such a stark demonstration that our national security interests are synonymous with our energy security. And here are—in this "perfect storm"—the various storm fronts that are coming together and colliding to produce some very ominous results for the American people, their families, and small businesses.

The travel season is heading into its annual peak as more and more Americans hit the road, and those numbers are higher than usual because of people's fear of flying or the aggravation, the stress of commercial air travel due to security concerns and desires.

Refineries are also beginning their annual changeover from winter fuels to specially formulated, cleaner burning summer fuels that cost more to produce. Those increased costs at refineries, that are already running at near capacity, will be passed on to the American consumer.

In recent weeks, the Israelis have taken strong action to defend themselves from the escalating growth of heinous suicide bombings in Israel.

In response to all of this, the dictator of Iraq, Saddam Hussein, has pledged to embargo Iraq's oil exports for 30 days or until Israel withdraws from Palestinian territories.

The Associated Press quoted Saddam as saying:

"The oppressive Zionist and American enemy has belittled the capabilities of the [Arab] nation."

Combine all of these factors together, and the price of gasoline has increased about 25 cents a gallon in just the last few weeks. This is the sharpest increase in a 4-week period since the year 1990, right before the gulf war.

The price of a barrel of oil has risen to about $26 a barrel as of yesterday, and many projections indicate the price will spike to more than $30 a barrel.

The problem is one of basic economics that a fourth grade student in Virginia would understand, or as the Presiding Officer would certainly agree, a fourth grade student in West Virginia as well. I hope that the Senate also understands this very basic, simple matter of high demand and inadequate supply. Even as the demand for oil is rising, supply is constrained this year because the nations in OPEC have cut production since the end of the year 2000 by a total of about 5 million barrels of oil per day.

The result is financial hardship for families and enterprises that pay more out of pocket for their basic transportation needs. It is a loaded weapon aimed at our economy, which appears to be moving slowly on the road to recovery.

I wholeheartedly support a balanced energy policy, including conservation and new, advanced technologies, such as hydrogen-fuel-cell-powered vehicles, electric vehicles, hybrid vehicles, and clean coal technology. We are the "Saudi Arabia of coal." I know the Chair shares my desire in working for clean coal technologies—and also solar photovoltaic technology.

But at the same time, we must increase our American-based production to become less reliant and dependent on foreign sources of oil.

Rising tensions in the Middle East will further increase our prices at the gas pump, damage job opportunities, and take more money from working people. This increased cost in fuel will ultimately cause an increase in the cost of goods and products, 95 percent of which come by truck to some store or directly to your home.

Please be aware that the United States continues to import nearly 1 million barrels a day from Saddam Hussein. This is the same man who turns around and compensates the families of suicide bombers at a rate of $25,000.

You could say that the compensation for 1 murderer is equivalent to about 900 barrels of oil that the United States and other nations buy from Saddam Hussein. We can no longer afford to let Saddam Hussein quite literally put us over the barrel.

At a time when Iraq is calling for an OPEC embargo on oil sales to America, environmentally safe production in a small and desolate place on the barren Arctic Plain on the North Slope of Alaska could alone replace more than 35 years of Iraqi oil imports. The potential is enormous for large oil reserves relatively near that of the current production at Prudhoe Bay— about 16 billion barrels. Conservative estimates state that ANWR has more oil than all of Texas.

I read that the Senator from Connecticut yesterday said it would take 10 years to get oil flowing from the North Slope of Alaska and this ANWR area. Let's assume it would take 10 years. Maybe this decision should have been made 10 years ago. Indeed, this Senate, in 1995, as well as the House, passed exploration permission legislation in 1995. Unfortunately, that legislation and that permission to explore ANWR was vetoed by the President in 1995. If that had not been vetoed, that oil would be flowing and we would not have as great a dependence on foreign oil, much less Saddam Hussein.

Also, there are groups of opponents. Many of those groups were also the opponents who were against the Prudhoe Bay production several decades ago. Thank goodness, reason and security prevailed and we are getting oil through the pipeline from Prudhoe Bay.

The reality is, with the infrastructure and the Trans-Alaska Pipeline less than about 50 miles away, just a few years of work are needed to get oil flowing from ANWR. The pipeline is already built. We just need to get that 50 mile span built from Prudhoe Bay to the exploration site at ANWR. It is not quite the magnitude of a project back in the 1970s.

The amount of oil we will be getting from there is about the same as what we could replace from 30 years of Saudi Arabian imports. And on top of it all, there are estimates—I will admit this is on the high side—of the creation of as many as 735,000 new jobs. The estimated oil at ANWR is valued at more than $300 billion, which could replace a large portion of foreign oil imports and clearly create hundreds of thousands of jobs for our economy.

Again, the North Slope of Alaska, the Arctic Plain, or ANWR, is not some mountainous, beautiful sanctuary. It is a flat, barren, cold, inhospitable place, and the small local population nearby is virtually unanimous in its desire to see the utilization of the resources beneath that frozen tundra. As it is very nearby, and similar to Prudhoe Bay, and as has been seen from studies, there will be no adverse impact on caribou or mosquitoes, which are plentiful in the summer, or other flora and fauna.

I support environmentally responsible exploration and production at ANWR to help at least ameliorate our dependence on OPEC. The announcement of curtailed exports by Iraq should remind us more than ever that our economy and national security will remain bound together as long as we allow tyrants and despots to control our destiny.

In addition to the Middle East, the political dispute in Venezuela has left their oil industry crippled as labor groups have staged a nationwide strike.

Simply put, we are entirely too dependent on foreign oil and we must expand our domestic production. We must also improve our energy security by identifying and developing new energy opportunities. Diversification of energy supplies is basic to our comprehensive national energy policy. We should encourage new, cooperative trade arrangements and new resources in willing prospects throughout the world.

All of these initiatives, discussions, and cooperative efforts are aimed at fulfilling just one part of our national energy policy, which is the diversification of our international sources of supply.

A commonsense, comprehensive, long-term energy plan will get us off this roller coaster of restrictive supply and demand that we have ridden for the past several decades. We must not allow the Saddam Husseins of the world to jerk us around and actually run that roller coaster.

President Bush's energy plan is comprehensive. It combines conservation and incentives for the development of alternative energy sources. I look forward to voting for tax incentives for alternative-fueled vehicles. It also includes increased domestic production. An energy policy without all of these components will not be effective.

We have a responsibility to the American people to address these challenges head on. If you think the situation is dire today, take a look just a short time from now into the future. Over the next 20 years, U.S. oil consumption is projected to increase by 33 percent and demand for electricity is projected to increase by 45 percent. Our dependence on foreign sources of oil will grow from 55 percent today to 64 percent by the year 2020. This compares to just 42 percent from foreign sources less than 10 years ago.

Clearly, we can see that something must be done, and soon. I am committed to working for commonsense solutions based upon sound science and the best available technologies so that all Americans can have affordable, reliable access to energy to fuel our motor vehicles, our homes, our farm operations, and our business operations across America.

I am also committed to making fuller use of the resources we have within our own borders in States that are supportive. While there may be oil off the coast of California, the people of California are opposed to oil development off their coast. Therefore, I respect their desires and would not support oil exploration off California.

In Alaska, Republicans, Democrats, Eskimos, Indians, all people are overwhelmingly in favor of production in ANWR.

There are other groups that support production on the North Slope of Alaska—groups such as the Vietnam Veterans Institute. I quote from them:

"War and international terrorism have again brought into sharp focus the heavy reliance of the U.S. on imported oil. During these times of crises, such reliance threatens our national security and economic well-being. … It is important that we develop domestic sources of oil."

Organized labor. This is from Jerry Hood of the International Brotherhood of Teamsters:

"America has gone too long without a solid energy plan. When energy costs rise, working families are the first to feel the pinch. The Senate should follow the example passed by the House and ease the burden by sending the President supply-based energy legislation to sign."

The Hispanic community. I quote from Mario Rodriguez, president of the United States-Mexico Chamber of Commerce:

"We urge the Senate leadership to pass comprehensive energy legislation. This is not a partisan issue. Millions of needy Hispanic families need your support now."

From Jewish organizations, Mort Zuckerman, chairman of the Conference of Presidents of Major American Jewish Organizations:

"The [Conference] at its general meeting on November 14th unanimously supported a resolution calling on Congress to act expeditiously to pass the energy bill that will serve to lessen our dependence on foreign sources of oil."

African-American groups. Harry Alford, chairman of the National Black Chamber of Commerce, states:

"Our growing membership reflects the opinion of more and more Americans all across the political spectrum that we must act now to end our dependence on foreign energy sources by addressing the nation's long-neglected energy needs."

And Bruce Josten of the U.S. Chamber of Commerce stated:

"The events of September 11 lend a new urgency to our efforts to increase domestic energy supplies and modernize our nation's energy infrastructure."

The point of all this is that it has broad, bipartisan support across the country, not just in Alaska. I also add that this is not simply a matter of our economic security our physical security is also at stake.

I challenge my colleagues to join Americans in this effort. Let's make America the most technologically advanced nation in the world for new sources of energy to propel our motor vehicles and to provide clean, efficient electricity. Let's also make sure we are less dependent upon unpredictable and, in some cases, threatening foreign sources of oil. Let's control our own destiny more than we have in the past. Let's move forward united for America's bright future.

[Congressional Record: S2556-2558]

" In Alaska, having been chairman of the Republican Senatorial Committee, looking at poll after poll last year, it is amazing how uniform the support is among the people of Alaska—Democrats, Republicans, Indians, Eskimos, and even in the sub-categorized iberals; liberals in Alaska are in favor of this pipeline. They understand it can be done in an environmentally sound way. It means jobs, revenues. And for us outside of Alaska, the lower 48, and Hawaii, this means energy security. "

ENERGY SECURITY AND ALASKA DRILLING

March 16, 2005

Mr. President, in listening to the debate, I will tell you what people in the real world care about and that is not process. What people care about, when you see them in the hallways, or anywhere across our country, they care about these high gasoline prices they are having to pay. I agree with the Senator from Washington, to some degree, that we do need to embrace a national energy policy that utilizes the advances of technology. We need more electricity being produced by clean coal technology, propulsion by fuel cell vehicles, and also we need to look at nuclear as a part of the mix, as opposed to natural gas for electricity base-load generation.

Rather than talk about process, let's talk about reality. The Senator from Massachusetts is talking about process that no one in the real world cares about. But what I understand is my own experience. I have been to the North Slope, Prudhoe Bay in late November. It was like the dark side of the moon. I also studied this over the years and have seen that Prudhoe Bay has development. I think it is a magnificent engineering feat. In the summer, it is full of mosquitoes, and at other times there are herds of animals that have to be fairly hardy animals to live up there.

So the argument ends up being, gosh, if there is a pipeline, there will be a gravel road. All of what happened in Prudhoe Bay has not had an adverse impact on the animals up there, or the mosquitoes, and if there is a gravel road in an area the size of Dulles Airport in a refuge the size of South Carolina, a few gravel roads won't have much impact. I know the occupant of the Chair, who is from South Carolina, knows that doesn't stop deer in his State. It certainly doesn't stop any other animals.

The reality is we have high gas prices, gasoline, and natural gas. It is affecting our travel and people in their homes. There are three reasons this amendment needs to stay and we get this revenue from this production. No. 1, security. We are overly dependent upon foreign sources of energy. We are being jerked around and sitting here reading e-mails to see what OPEC is going to do. Are they going to increase production by a few hundred thousand barrels? What impact will that have? Yes, other countries, such as India and China, are taking coal and taking energy, such as oil.

But the point is we should be less dependent and reliant for our own security on OPEC and Venezuela and all these different countries, primarily in the Middle East, for our own security. We are presently 58-percent dependent upon foreign oil. It is going to go up to 68 percent in the next 15 years. That is the estimate.

Second, this is for jobs. Jobs will be created. Hundreds of thousands of jobs in everything from manufacturing, mining, trade, services, construction, and others. It is going to have an impact mostly on Alaska, but also across the country. That is good for our country as well.

Talking about this being Yellowstone, I would not open up exploration at Yellowstone. Nobody is suggesting that. The west coast of Florida, the people there, if they want to have a reasonable distance from oil production that doesn't draw the line all the way to Mississippi and Louisiana, respect the will of the people of the west coast of Florida. If the people of Charleston, SC, don't want drilling off the coast of South Carolina, we ought to respect those people.

In Alaska, having been chairman of the Republican Senatorial Committee, looking at poll after poll last year, it is amazing how uniform the support is among the people of Alaska—Democrats, Republicans, Indians, Eskimos, and even in the sub-categorized liberals; liberals in Alaska are in favor of this pipeline. They understand it can be done in an environmentally sound way. It means jobs, revenues. And for us outside of Alaska, the lower 48, and Hawaii, this means energy security.

Finally, in addition to security and jobs, there is competitiveness. This country needs to have a reliable, affordable source of energy, whether that is oil or natural gas. Many fertilizer and chemical manufacturers, paper, plastic—even in Danville, VA, where they manufacture tires at a Goodyear plant, they are concerned about the skyrocketing costs of natural gas. Natural gas is available in other countries around the world at a more affordable price. They are competing to get Airbus airplane tires. They got the contract, but obviously tires can be made in Southeast Asia, or elsewhere in the world.

It is important for our competitiveness that we have a more stable and affordable energy supply. So I ask you all, my colleagues, to do what is right for the security of this country and jobs for Americans and, most important, for the competitiveness of our country. Support what the Budget Committee has done. Let's use those resources on the North Slope of Alaska for American job security and competitiveness and do what is right by the people in the real world, who would like to see us act, as opposed to worrying about what people in OPEC say about our gas prices.

[Congressional Record: S2771]

“Today's system has failed to make the elections more competitive. The current system hurts voters in our Republic by forcing more and more committees and contributions and political activists to operate outside the system where they are unaccountable and, consequently, more irresponsible and less honest.”

CAMPAIGN FINANCE REFORM

March 27, 2001

M r. President, and Members of the Senate, I rise in support of the Thompson amendment. I have listened to the debate on this issue for the last several days, and I have listened to the many different points of view expressed here. There is quite a spectrum of opinion. On one side of the spectrum, there are those—and they had 40 votes—who want to limit First Amendment rights and, in fact, voted for a Constitutional amendment to do just that. I actually commend the Senator from South Carolina, Mr. Hollings, for at least recognizing that many of these proposals, including the McCain-Feingold bill, have the effect of restricting First Amendment rights, which is part of the Bill of Rights. Nevertheless, that is their view.

On that side of the spectrum, there are also those who want the taxpayers to pay for elections, which would be the result if you actually limited First Amendment rights. They honestly believe that is the approach to take. I find myself on the other end of the spectrum, as one who believes very much in the Bill of Rights. After all, it was first authored by George Mason in the Virginia

Declaration of Rights. I think the First Amendment, as well as all of the Bill of Rights, is very important for all Americans. My view is that what we ought to have is more freedom; the maximum amount of individual freedom, and the maximum amount of accountability and honesty in elections, and having contributions made voluntarily as opposed to being taken out of tax money.

All the various amendments that have been offered today, and probably will be offered in the next few days, have as their purpose various restrictions or subterfuge to these two different points of view.

I have been a candidate for statewide office in Virginia twice. Last year, I ran statewide for the U.S. Senate under the Federal election laws. I also ran for Governor statewide, obviously, under Virginia's laws that are based upon the principles of freedom. In my view, the current Federal election laws are overly restrictive. They are bureaucratic, antiquated, and they are contrary to the principles of individual freedom, accountability and, yes, contrary to the concepts of honesty.

I have been working on an amendment with the Senator from Texas, Mr. Gramm, on what we call the Political Freedom and Accountability Act. I don't know if we will offer that amendment, but this looks like an opportunity to be in support of something that is at least going in that same direction. I have stood by my guiding principles on vote after vote during this debate. Sometimes I do not agree with the Senator from Kentucky on an amendment; to his and my chagrin, because I consider the professor someone very knowledgeable on this subject. Nonetheless, I am trying to advocate greater freedom and greater accountability.

What I am trying to do is make sure that in this debate we are advancing the ideas of freedom of exchange of ideas, freedom of political expression and increasing participation to the maximum extent possible. And equally important are the concepts of accountability and honesty.

First, the issue of freedom. The current laws and limits are clearly out of date. There is no one who can argue that these laws, the current restriction on direct contributions to candidates, are anything but completely antiquated and out of date. Let's take some examples. When TV reporters ask me what kind of reforms do I want, I tell them greater freedom, greater accountability, and to get these Federal laws up to date. I ask the TV reporters: Will you please, in your reporting of this issue, say what it cost to run a 30-second ad in 1974 when these laws were put into effect versus what you charge today for a TV ad.

Well, I am never home enough to watch TV anymore since I have joined the Senate, so maybe they told us. Nevertheless, we did our own research. The average cost of just producing a 30-second commercial has increased seven times, from $4,000 to $28,000. The cost of stamps—because we do send mailings out has increased. The cost of a first-class stamp in 1974 was 10 cents. Today, it is 34 cents, and rising. So that is over three times as much.

The cost of airing a 30-second television advertisement per 1,000 homes has escalated from $2 in 1974 to $11 in 1997. That is fivefold increase.

Candidates are today running in larger districts. There are more people in congressional districts, obviously, than before. There are more people in the United States of America. The voting-age population increased from 141 million in 1974 to over 200 million in 1998.

The reality is that the limits in the Thompson amendment don't even catch up with the increase in costs.

The Thompson amendment is a very modest approach of trying to get the Federal election laws more in line with what are the costs of campaigns.

The accountability and honesty aspect of this amendment is important because I think the current situation has improper disclosure; very poor disclosure and subterfuge. As far as disclosure is concerned, one can get a contribution of $1,000 on July 2 and it is not disclosed until late October under the current law. I very much agree with the efforts of the Senator from Louisiana, Ms. Landrieu, to get more prompt disclosure, and that needs to be done.

The contribution limits also force a greater use of soft money. People are all so upset about soft money going to political parties. Why is that being done? Because the cost of campaigns are increasing for all those demographic features and facts I just enunciated. The fact is, you need more money to run campaigns to get your messages out.

If an individual desired to part with $5,000, which is right much money for most people, but they believe so much in a candidate that they want to give $5,000, right now they would have to give $1,000 to the candidate. That would be disclosed, maybe belatedly but it would be disclosed. Then they would have to give $4,000 to a political party that would run ads, run mailings, whatever they would do to help that candidate.

The point is that $4,000, in this example, would not have the same accountability. It would not have the same scrutiny. Fred Smith may be a controversial character. It is one thing for him to give $1,000 and then $4,000 to the party, but it is all $5,000 to candidate B and you say: Gosh, candidate

B has gotten all this money from Fred Smith. But really it only shows up as $1,000 because the rest has gone to the Democratic Party or the Republican Party or some other organization. Therefore, you are losing that accountability and the true honesty in a campaign that you want to have and the scrutiny that a candidate should have for getting contributions from individuals.

It is my view that we need to return responsibility for campaigns to the candidates. We are getting swamped. At least we were swamped—and I know this was not unique to Virginia last year—with these outside groups that are contributing to our campaigns. Mr. President, $5 million, at least the best we can determine, was spent not just by the Democratic Party running ads contrary to my campaign or Republicans running ads in favor of my campaign or in opposition to my opponent, but these independent expenditures—handgun control, attack TV ads, donor undisclosed; Sierra Club running attack ads, radio ads, voter guides, donors undisclosed; pro-abortion groups, dirty dozen ads against us—all these ads and they are all undisclosed. There are people all upset with this. That is part of democracy. That is part of free expression. It would be nice if there would be a constitutional way to disclose those individuals, but that is apparently unconstitutional.

The point is, you end up having to answer those ads. People think: You want to do all sorts of sordid things I will not repeat, but nevertheless you have to get the money to make sure you are getting your positive, constructive message out or setting the record straight.

With these limits, you end up having to raise money through political parties to combat these ads which, as much as I did not like them, they have a right to do. And I will defend the rights of these groups or any other groups to run those ads and have their free expression and political participation.

The point of the Thompson amendment is people are allowed to contribute more directly to a candidate. The candidate is held more responsible and accountable, and to the extent that you can get more direct contributions, it alleviates, negates, and diminishes the need to be using political parties as a subterfuge or a conduit to get the money you need to set the record straight.

Current Federal laws in many cases—one says: Look at how wonderful they are. It is amazing to me people think that, but nevertheless that is their view. They are so unaccountable in so many ways, and by limiting hard dollars, so to speak, or direct contributions, you are back with PACs. ...

I think the contribution limits definitely create a dependency on soft money, thereby the corollary logically is that by increasing the direct contributions on hard limits, it decreases the necessity. It is pure commonsense logic, at least for those of us who have run under a system of freedom such as that in Virginia.

The other matter is contribution limits also prohibit candidates, except those with personal wealth, from acquiring a stake from which to launch a campaign. We went through this whole debate about what happens when you have millionaire candidates and thereby raise the limits for those candidates, and so forth. Gosh, if you did not have any limits, you would not have to worry about this.

Again, at least the amendment of the Senator from Tennessee addresses that in that we want to encourage more political participation in speech rather than limiting it. We ought to be promoting competition. We ought to be promoting freedom and a more informed electorate, which we would get with the amendment of the Senator from Tennessee. We want to enable any law-abiding American citizen to run for office.

Had the current limits been in place in 1968, Eugene McCarthy never would have been able to mount his effort against President Johnson.

Today's system has failed to make the elections more competitive. The current system hurts voters in our Republic by forcing more and more committees and contributions and political activists to operate outside the system where they are unaccountable and, consequently, more irresponsible and less honest.

I, of course, want to repeal the hard limits, but nevertheless, by increasing these limits, we can open up the political system. Challengers need to raise a great deal of money as quickly as possible to have any real chance of success. The current system, with its very stringent limits, prevents a challenger from raising the funds he or she needs, and I saw that in 1993 when I was running for Governor.

One may say: Gosh, this is all wonderful theory from the Senator from Virginia. You can look at Virginia as a test case of freedom and accountability. People say, sure, they have plenty of disagreements between the legislative and executive branch and between Democrats and Republicans, but you have honest Government in Virginia. If there is anybody giving large contributions, I guarantee you, boy that is scrutinized and there is a lot of answering to do for large contributions. Indeed, it may not be worth the bad press you get for accepting a large contribution.

Again, if you look at Virginia—which has a system where we have no contribution limits and better disclosure—Virginia right now has a Governor whose father was a butcher. His predecessor was a son of a former football coach. The predecessor to that Governor was a grandson of slaves. Virginia's system gives equal opportunity to all. Virginia has a record of which we can be proud.

The amendment of the Senator from Tennessee, while not ideal and exactly like Virginia, it is one that at least increases freedom—freedom of participation, freedom of expression, and coupled with other amendments, such as the amendment of the Senator from Louisiana on disclosure, brings greater honesty.

I urge my fellow Senators to support this amendment. It is a reasonable improvement, it is greater freedom, it is greater accountability, and it is greater honesty for the people of America. I yield back what moments I have remaining.

[Congressional Record: S2962-2963]

" The implications of an abused tort system on the American economy are of legitimate concern. While there is no doubt that many class action lawsuits are legitimate, the inadequacies of the system have resulted in frequent abuses. And the increased cost to businesses has an enormous impact—tying the hands of businesses and restricting their ability to expand, provide additional jobs, or contribute to the economy. "

TORT REFORM

February 10, 2005

Mr. President, I rise today in support of the Class Action Fairness Act.

This legislation we are considering today is crucial to ensuring that there is fairness in our courtrooms, that claimants receive the judicial consideration they deserve, and that the American economy and small businesses are able to stay competitive.

This class action reform legislation is primarily designed to allow defendants to move a class action lawsuit from State court to Federal court when there is diversity or citizens from different States involved in the litigation. This concept is as old as our Republic. No one will be denied access to the courts. It is simply allowing most litigants to find the most appropriate court to decide the case. In significant cases with diversity, the Federal courts are the proper choice.

We have heard about cases where lawyers shop around to find courts in particular counties that have a proven track record of being sympathetic to class action lawsuits with absurdly large judgments. When justice arbitrarily hinges on what county in which a case is tried, that is not fair.

A recent study found that 89 percent of Americans believe the legal system is in need of reform. The statistics are indeed alarming: Over the past decade, the number of class action lawsuits has increased by over 1,000 percent nationwide. And the cost of the U.S. tort system has increased one hundred fold over the last 50 years. Lloyd's of London estimates that the tort system cost $205 billion in 2001, or $721 per U.S. citizen. Most importantly, Lloyd's estimates this number to rise to $298 billion by this year. At current levels, U.S. tort costs are equivalent to a five percent tax on wages.

The implications of an abused tort system on the American economy are of legitimate concern. While there is no doubt that many class action lawsuits are legitimate, the inadequacies of the system have resulted in frequent abuses. And the increased cost to businesses has an enormous impact—tying the hands of businesses and restricting their ability to expand, provide additional jobs, or contribute to the economy. Even the threat of class action lawsuits forces businesses to spend millions of dollars. Defendants face the risk of a single judgment in the tens of millions or even billions of dollars, simply because a State court judge has rushed to certify a class without proper review. The risk of a single, bankrupting award often forces defendants to settle the case with sizable payments even when the defendant has meritorious defenses.

Believe it or not, some opponents of the Class Action Fairness Act are still urging that the current class action system works well and that class action reform is unnecessary. Apparently, they do not think it is a problem when consumers take home 50-cent coupons to compensate them for their injuries, while their lawyers pocket millions in cash. Take for example a case against Blockbuster, Inc., where customers alleged they were charged excessive late fees for video rentals. These customers received $1 coupons while their attorneys received over $9 million. Or when one State court prevents citizens from litigating their claims under the law of their home State. Or when attorneys file the same lawsuit in dozens of State courts across the country and file the same lawsuit in a race to see which judge will certify the fastest and broadest class.

In fact, numerous studies have documented class action abuses taking place in a small number of "magnet" State courts, and by now, it is beyond legitimate debate that our class action system is in shambles. As the *Washington Post* editorial page has noted, "[n]o portion of the American civil justice system is more of a mess than the world of class action."

A RAND Institute for Civil Justice, ICJ, Study on U.S. class actions released at the end of 1999 empirically confirms what has long been widely believed—State court consumer class actions primarily benefit lawyers, not the consumers on whose behalf the actions ostensibly are brought. Case studies in the ICJ piece confirm that in State court consumer class actions— that is, cases not involving personal injury claims—the fees received by attorneys are typically larger than the total amount of monetary benefits paid to all of the class members combined. In short, the lawyers are the primary beneficiaries. The ICJ Study contains no data indicating that this problem exists in Federal court class actions.

If we do not pass this vital legislation, the class action process will remain a system ripe for exploitation, and the harm to the fundamental fairness of the civil justice system will continue to grow. Excessive and frivolous class action lawsuits stifle innovation, discourage risk-taking, and harm the entrepreneurship that drives our Nation's economic growth and job creation.

This commonsense, bipartisan legislation will help alleviate the dramatic effects that have resulted from an abuse of the class action system. This legislation ensures that legitimate class action cases are given full consideration and that prevailing plaintiffs receive the compensation they deserve. Americans deserve to have a judicial system that is effective and efficient, and, most importantly, fair—this legislation goes a long way toward accomplishing these objectives. I urge my colleagues to support this legislation. In the 108th Congress, this legislation came up one vote short. We now have four more Senators on our side of the aisle, so I am confident in its success in the 109th Congress. This is a success that people in States desire, and it will be a promise kept.

[Congressional Record: S1238-1239]

" We saw in the 2000 election that some voters in our armed services were not able to participate or have their votes counted; in effect, not being able to vote for their prospective Commander in Chief. … These are people who honorably serve our country, and we want to make sure the votes they cast for their elected officials are counted. "

Voting Rights

February 14, 2002

Mr. President, we are now debating the issue of voting rights. Let's put it in perspective. Yesterday evening, an amendment offered by Senator Allard of Colorado, which I cosponsored, was adopted. It is a very good amendment. It improves and clarifies the laws surrounding voting by those who serve in the military.

Senator Allard's amendment is certainly needed. We saw in the 2000 election that some voters in our armed services were not able to participate or have their votes counted; in effect, not being able to vote for their prospective Commander in Chief.

The issues we are discussing today are very important, but one of the more important improvements was addressing the needs of our military voters. These are people who honorably serve our country, and we want to make sure the votes they cast for their elected officials are counted. Indeed, their service to protect our freedoms should not diminish their rights to participate in representative democracy.

Senator Allard's amendment is an effort to make sure those votes are cast. Some of the postmark problems make no sense when people are overseas and on ships. It also makes sure State and local jurisdictions are better informed of performing their important duties in administering elections fairly.

All of this recognizes the important role of the localities and the States in making sure the elections are administered fairly and, indeed, making sure those who serve overseas can exercise their constitutional right to vote in Federal elections.

Who does the Allard amendment apply to? It applies to over 2.7 million members of the military and their families who are stationed away from their home today in service to the people and the principles of our Republic.

Many of these men and women are residents of the Commonwealth of Virginia, the birthplace of American liberty and indeed home of the first legislative body in the western hemisphere which was formed in 1619, long before this body was formed.

I was proud to lend my name and my voice to Senator Allard's amendment because it ensures that those who serve our country honorably and with distinction have their voices heard, not just in Virginia but in every State of the Union.

We go from protecting those who honorably serve to a debate on this pending amendment, which advocates undesirable Federal meddling into the so-called voting rights of convicted felons. Indeed, throughout the Senate, our colleagues care about people across the spectrum of responsibility, from those citizens who are more responsible to even those who are less responsible.

I refer my colleagues to an article recently published in the *Fredericksburg Free Lance-Star* on February 5 of this year which deals with the issue of voting rights for felons in Virginia and has been mentioned by both its proponents and its opponents. The various States have differing approaches to the restoration of voting rights or any rights to those who have been convicted of felonies.

Now I will say that in Virginia—before I get to this article—having been Governor of Virginia, I took the responsibility very seriously when reviewing the petitions of those who had been convicted of felonies. It struck me in a very interesting way. In the midst of a campaign, I was down in Buchanan County, which is far southwestern Virginia. It is on the Kentucky/West Virginia border. It is a coal county. I was campaigning early in my campaign for Governor at this country store called Pentley's, which, sadly, has since closed down. At any rate, I went in there shaking hands, handing out cards. It was such a memorable event in that Mrs. Pentley, the lady who ran the store, thought it was wonderful that a candidate for statewide office actually came to her store, in Buchanan County. She said: You are the most famous person who has come here since the guy who invented 10,000 flushes came here, because he was on TV and we did not have enough money at the time to be on TV.

As I left that store all charged up because she put my little card up, there was a fellow leaning up against the drink machine where the ice is kept, and he said: "I like you. You are a good guy."

I said: "Well, thank you. I hope you will vote for me."

He said: "Well, I cannot."

I said: "Well, why not? Are you not registered?"

"No, I am not registered."

I said: "Why not?"

He said: "I cannot get registered."

I said: "Of course you can. What is your excuse? What are you, a convicted felon?"

He said: "Yes."

I said: "Okay. Well, talk to your friends and neighbors and folks you might influence."

With this, I left and I told this story all around Virginia.

Fortunately, I was elected by the good people of Virginia to serve as Governor, and I thought it was always important to take the Governor's office to the people, so I said: Let's go back to Pentley's Store and thank Mrs. Pentley for all her inspiration. Mrs. Pentley does not know how much I would talk about her.

We were in an RV. As we got out of the RV—this was 2 or 3 years later—there was this same fellow who looked as if he had grown some teeth and had a nicer shirt, one that did not have a hole in it. He said: "Do you remember me?"

I said: "I sure do. I do remember you. You are looking good today."

He said: "I voted for you."

When you win an election, everyone says they voted for you.

I said: "I do remember you. You told me you were a convicted felon. I know you could not have voted for me."

He said: "But I did."

I said: "What happened? Did Governor Wilder restore your voting rights?"

He said: "Yes, he did, and I voted for you."

That is a personal story about treating everyone with dignity and respect. Who would have known that Governor Wilder, who is not in the same party I am, would have restored this gentleman's right to vote before the election and he voted for me?

In Virginia, I would look at these situations very seriously, not just because of this gentleman in Buchanan County but because those who petitioned me would talk about their sacred right to vote.

Let's look at how Virginia is compared to other States. Virginia is 1 of 10 States that permanently prevent—and this is according to the *Fredericksburg Free Lance-Star* in Fredericksburg—ex-felons from voting. Alabama, Delaware, Florida, Iowa, Kentucky, Mississippi, Nevada, New Mexico, and Wyoming are others. Maryland cuts it off for second-time felons. That does not mean their rights can never be restored. Their rights can be restored.

In Virginia, this is not an issue of first impression. It is being debated now as it has been for many years. In fact, in 1982, in Virginia, there was a referendum asking voters to let the State legislature, rather than the Governor, restore the voting rights of felons. The people of Virginia voted on whether or not to ease this process, which I will say is fairly cumbersome and it failed by nearly 300,000 votes.

This amendment, if it were to become law, would abrogate the express will of the people of Virginia and also the will of many other States, whether it is by a referendum or by their elected State legislatures.

In the Commonwealth of Virginia, the legislature recommended streamlining the petition process for nonviolent felons who did their time, finished probation, and waited another 5 years. It would have allowed the local circuit court to restore those rights, taking that burden off the Governor.

Of course, many ex-felons did get their rights back. There is the record of my successor, he restored the rights of 210 people during his 4-year term. That is less than half of what was restored during the previous three administrations. While I was Governor, I restored 459 ex-felons' rights to vote.

The understanding of who is best in a position to administer these laws and determine when ex-felons ought to have their rights restored, clearly lies with the States. This amendment, if passed, would preempt the States with regard to this important function.

The Ford-Carter Commission agrees with this assessment. The Commission concluded: We doubt Congress has the constitutional power to legislate a Federal prescription on States prohibiting felons from voting.

Virginia allows ex-felons to petition for restoration of voting rights 5 years after they have completed all of their probation or all of their parole. If they have been convicted of a drug offense, it is 7 years, because there are people who not only commit crimes, but they repeat crimes. Also, if the offense is related to drugs, you want to make sure they are completely off their addiction to drugs.

The things most Governors would look at, regardless of party, is what kind of life has the ex-felon led since serving their time? I would consider whether or not they were involved in wholesome community-based activities, or just leading the life of a law-abiding citizen and not committing any crimes.

Governors will want to see what kind of a positive life the person has led since leaving prison. The petitioner would oftentimes write to me explaining why they wanted their rights restored. As Governor I considered that in my assessment of each individual case as well.

Another thing missing from this amendment is the issue of restitution and court costs. I always looked at restitution and court costs in my assessment.

In Virginia, I cared a great deal about restitution and court costs. With regard to some of these folks, you would say, well, these are not important crimes. But embezzlement, to the extent there can be restitution, that is usually ordered by a judge in sentencing. You would want to see if restitution has been made. You would want to see if they have paid back their court costs. If it were a robbery or a burglary, you would want to see if restitution has been made. There are certain situations where, as a condition of probation or suspension of a sentence, they want medical costs associated with the rape or malicious wounding to be paid.

None of that is in this amendment. It is only probation and the parole. But restitution and the payment of court costs ought to be considered. At least I considered it as Governor.

The reason why people want rights restored is interesting. Generally, there are three categories. One is they want to feel like a full-fledged citizen again. They have led a good life. They want to be part of the community. Some of it was job-related. They have not had their rights restored. They wanted their kids to feel better about themselves.

A second reason they want to vote is to participate in elections. The third reason, as often as the rest, is to go hunting. When you lose your rights, you lose your right to carry a firearm. I suppose you could throw rocks at deer, but usually people want a shotgun or a rifle to go deer or duck hunting.

Now the Federal Government in this amendment is saying that the States will have to restore rights, notwithstanding the will of the people, notwithstanding the prerogatives of their duly elected representatives in the legislature. For Federal elections only, you will have to allow them to vote.

In the Commonwealth of Virginia, the Commonwealth of Kentucky, and maybe a few other States, our State elections are different than Federal elections. You will need two sets of registration for the State elections and local elections. To keep the laws in place in Virginia or any other State, there are dual roles for registered voters that would be a cost to the States and localities.

In Virginia, where Federal elections do not run at the same time as State elections, this is probably not too big of an issue. But imagine in the States where Federal elections and State elections are conducted at the same time. That is undoubtedly true in over 40 States. There will be two sets of ballots for people to use when they vote. If they want to keep their rights and prerogatives and reflect the desires of the people of their State, two ballots will be needed. When you have Federal and State elections, there are names of Presidential candidates, candidates for Congress, maybe the Senate, along with State legislators, Governor, Lieutenant Governor, whoever else is being elected. We will need a separate ballot for those who have the right to vote in State and Federal, and a separate ballot for those only in Federal elections. In effect, what we would need at the polling place is a separate voting booth.

I guess we would have an ex-felon voting booth where they would only vote in Federal elections, while the vast majority of the other voters would vote in the others.

This causes a great deal of unnecessary cost and imposes many impractical problems on the State. The goal of the bill is to help voting fairness in the States, respecting the rights of States, not putting on unfounded mandates as has been done previously. This amendment will cause consternation and confusion.

Most importantly, understanding the basic jurisdiction, I object to this amendment in that it usurps the rights of the States. It usurps and preempts and dictates contrary to the will of the people not only of the Commonwealth of Virginia but it exceeds the scope and breadth of what the Federal Government should be involved in.

I hope my colleagues will allow this issue to be properly debated in the way the framers of our Constitution thought it should be debated and decided. That is, in the State legislatures, as opposed to meddling from the Federal Government.

We care about the voting of military personnel overseas. I don't see where we have any business meddling in trying to get ex-felons the right to vote.

[Congressional Record: S805-807]

"Police reports and Federal felon surveys have consistently shown that so-called assault weapons are used in only 1 to 2 percent of violent crimes. Crime victim surveys indicate the figure is only one-quarter of 1 percent, 0.25. Murders with knives, clubs and hands outnumber those with assault weapons by over 20-to-1. Put another way, notwithstanding this 10-year ban of 19 firearms, criminals continue to commit criminal acts, they just do so with other weapons; with other guns, knives or objects."

GUN RIGHTS AND FIREARM LIABILITY LITIGATION

March 1, 2004

M r. President, S. 1805, which we are in the midst of debating, is good legislation and I am a cosponsor of this bill. It will help curb frivolous litigation against a lawful American industry and the thousands of workers it employs. Imagine if General Motors were to be held liable for every accident caused by a reckless or drunk driver. Likewise, businesses legally engaged in manufacturing, importing or selling firearms should not be liable for the harm caused by people who use that firearm in an unsafe or criminal manner. This legislation does carefully preserve the right of individuals to have their day in court with civil liability actions for injury or danger caused by negligence or defective product, a standard in product liability law.

Adding amendments such as an extension of the assault weapons ban threatens the chances of this important legislation ever becoming law. This bill is too important to be saddled with "poison pill" amendments.

Four years ago, in the midst of the 2000 election, I said that my goal in fighting criminals was to enforce, not repeal, existing laws. And, indeed, in Virginia we have seen that incarcerating violent felons is the best crime reduction policy. I would support reauthorization of the assault weapons ban in its current form if this legislation had proven effective in reducing violent crime. I have reviewed the thoughtful claims and extensive assertions of proponents and opponents of this law. I have concluded, after a review of the evidence, that this symbolic ban of 19 firearms chosen for cosmetic reasons is a meaningless, toothless law that has virtually no impact on crime. I have decided, therefore, to vote against extension of the assault weapons ban.

Police reports and Federal felon surveys have consistently shown that so-called assault weapons are used in only 1 to 2 percent of violent crimes. Crime victim surveys indicate the figure is only one-quarter of 1 percent, 0.25. Murders with knives, clubs and hands outnumber those with assault weapons by over 20-to-1.

Put another way, notwithstanding this 10-year ban of 19 firearms, criminals continue to commit criminal acts, they just do so with other weapons; with other guns, knives or objects.

The simple fact is that the assault weapons ban only attacks the cosmetic features of a gun, banning some guns even though they function exactly the same as hundreds of other semi-automatic firearms.

It is also worth noting that we are not talking about the fully automatic firearms or machine guns that many Americans view as assault weapons—the Uzi and the AK-47—they were already banned by previous laws. Nor are we talking about any firearms that are readily or easily converted to fully automatic firearms. Sale of such firearms is already banned under current federal law.

I recently watched a CNN interview that showed an individual firing a gun that was banned under the 1994 law and a gun that is readily available today. Both guns produced the same results with the same impact. The only difference is that one had a different type of grip, stock or bayonet lock than the other. Therefore, the banning of these accessories is purely cosmetic. The focus should be on criminals not guns, and it should be on programs that work, like Project Exile and the Abolition of Parole.

I am also concerned that by reauthorizing this gun ban legislation, it will serve as a platform inviting added restrictions on Second Amendment rights. The current law, then, only makes sense if the ultimate goal it is to ban more and more guns in the future, something I cannot support. This can be seen in several proposals and amendments now before Congress to expand the current assault weapons ban proposals that permanently ban a large number of guns that citizens lawfully use for competition, hunting or self-defense. I have a long and consistent record of supporting the rights of Virginians and Americans to protect their families and themselves, and I am committed to protecting those rights of law-abiding American citizens.

[Congressional Record: S1928]

"By imposing harsh, unprecedented penalties upon Microsoft, the [E.U.] Commission has extended its view of competition and regulation beyond Europe and onto the United States—to the detriment of U.S. laws, industry and consumers."

ANTITRUST LAW AND AMERICAN SOVEREIGNTY

March 23, 2004

Mr. President, I rise to address the European Commission's antitrust action against Microsoft. It is my understanding that antitrust authorities for the European Union member nations have given European Competition Commissioner Mario Monti their unanimous backing for a formal commission finding that Microsoft abused its market share of its Windows operating system for personal computers to leverage its way into related markets for networking and multimedia software. It is expected that the European Commission will hand down a formal decision finding that Microsoft is in violation of European Union antitrust laws.

By imposing harsh, unprecedented penalties upon Microsoft, the Commission has extended its view of competition and regulation beyond Europe and onto the United States—to the detriment of U.S. laws, industry and consumers.

For many years, the European Union and its member states have criticized the United States for adopting laws and regulations that, in the view of

European policymakers, have had an extraterritorial reach. The European Commission in particular has consistently urged the United States to ensure that its legal determinations do not intrude into European affairs. We now have a clear example of the European Union not practicing what they preach.

If the Commission rules that Microsoft is in violation of European Union antitrust laws, it will undercut the settlement that was so carefully and painstakingly crafted with Microsoft by the U.S. Department of Justice and several state antitrust authorities. There can be no question that the U.S. Government was entitled to take the lead in this matter—Microsoft is a U.S. company, many if not all of the complaining companies in the EU case are American, and all of the relevant design decisions took place here. I would hope that if the Commission were cognizant of America's legitimate interests in this matter, it would act in a manner that complemented the U.S. settlement. I fear the Commission has selected a path that places its resolution of this case in direct conflict with ours.

This is not the only example of the Commission's overreaching in this case. In recent negotiations with Microsoft, the European Commission demanded that Microsoft agree to ensure that computer manufacturers who sell pre-installed versions of Windows also install three competing media players—an obligation that the Commission insisted on imposing not just within the EU, but globally. In spite of its objections to these requirements, Microsoft agreed to the Commission's approach in order to reach a settlement. I understand the Commission proposes to impose a fine of over $610 million on Microsoft—higher than any fine in the Commission's history. It has been suggested that the amount of this fine was based not only on Microsoft's conduct in the EU, but in the United States and elsewhere as well. One can only conclude that the Commission was not satisfied with how U.S. antitrust authorities and courts resolved the case against Microsoft, and therefore decided to act as a kind of supra-national competition authority by fining Microsoft for its conduct worldwide.

The Commission's proposed ruling, as well as its negotiation tactics, is unprecedented in its scope. By to fine Microsoft for purported anticompetitive conduct and injuries in the United States, the European Commission is directly challenging the adequacy of the United States' own antitrust laws, including the settlement that Microsoft and U.S. authorities reached in the U.S. proceedings. In fact, the obligations proposed to be imposed on Microsoft by the Commission are precisely the type that the U.S. District

Court and the U.S. Department of Justice rejected as undermining consumer welfare.

It is incumbent on the Departments of State and Justice to stand up not only for an important American company but more importantly for legitimate U.S. jurisdiction over alleged anticompetitive behavior in the United States. The U.S. and the EU are signatories to a 1991 comity agreement on antitrust issues which requires that one government defer to the other if the principal issues being investigated involve companies of one of the parties. Here, the EU is investigating a U.S. company based on complaints from other U.S. companies. If the U.S. Government does not make a clear and strong statement objecting to the EU's extraterritorial approach, we will lose influence and credibility for years to come to the detriment of all U.S. industry, as well as to U.S. consumers.

[Congressional Record: S2992-2993]

" This International Criminal Court, in fact, would be in a position to punish individual American officials for the foreign policy and military actions of the United States and would not offer even minimum guarantees afforded in the Bill of Rights to any defendants before it. "

INTERNATIONAL CRIMINAL COURT: THREAT TO AMERICAN SOVEREIGNTY

September 10, 2001

Mr. President, I rise in support of the amendment of our colleague, Senator Craig of Idaho, of which I am a cosponsor. I listened very carefully to the eloquent words of the Senator from Connecticut, Mr. Dodd, and his arguments in opposition to this amendment. In my view, the proposed International Criminal Court is a threat to the sovereignty of the United States and our individual God-given rights that are protected in the Constitution of the United States and in the constitutions and laws of several states. President Clinton, in my view, made a serious mistake when he signed the Rome treaty in the waning days of his administration. That treaty, which would establish a permanent international criminal court, creates a number of undesirable, unprecedented challenges for the people of the United States. The ICC will have the power to investigate and prosecute a series of international criminal offenses such as crimes against humanity, heretofore enforceable only in national courts or tribunals of limited application which have broad international support, such as the Nuremberg trials, which Senator Dodd brought up.

Obviously, everyone here thinks the Nazis should be prosecuted.

We do support, obviously, the tribunal that is trying Milosevic right at this moment. The International Court in The Hague is the proper approach, which does not impinge upon our sovereignty.

Senator Dodd, in arguing against this amendment, did mention he would oppose the Rome treaty as written if we were going to be voting on it at this moment. But if the Senate were to ratify this ill-advised treaty, this International Criminal Court would have the authority to try to punish Americans for alleged offenses abroad or in the United States, and that Court will be entirely unaccountable for its actions.

This International Criminal Court, in fact, would be in a position to punish individual American officials for the foreign policy and military actions of the United States and would not offer even minimum guarantees afforded in the Bill of Rights to any defendants before it.

At the heart of the ICC is an independent prosecutor accountable to no one. The international prosecutor is empowered to enforce justice as that prosecutor sees fit. If the international prosecutor believes that a local trial in our U.S. courts has been inadequate, he or she is authorized to indict an alleged human rights abuser and demand a new international trial. The international prosecutor may think a local pardon or an amnesty or a finding of not guilty was improper. That international prosecutor can ignore that finding.

What this authority symbolizes is the theory that all nations, including constitutional democracies, should surrender their sovereignty to the altar of international control.

Control of our own courts is one of our most cherished internal decisions about justice and order in our civilization. The United States was founded on the basic principle that the people of the States and our country have the right to govern themselves and chart their own course. The elected officials in the United States, as well as our military and citizenry at large, are ultimately responsible to the legal and political institutions established by our Federal and State constitutions, which reflect the values and the sovereignty of the American people.

The Rome treaty would erect an institution in the form of the ICC that would claim authority superior to that of the Federal Government and the States and superior to the American voters themselves. This Court would assert the ultimate authority to determine whether the elected officials of the United States as well as any other American citizen have acted unlawfully on any particular occasion.

In this, the Rome treaty is fundamentally inconsistent with the first tenet of our American Republic, that anyone who exercises power must be responsible for its use to those subject to that power. In our country, the Government derives its just powers from the consent of the people. That is foundational and fundamental.

The values of the ICC's prosecutor and judges are unlikely to be the same values of those of the United States. The Rome treaty has been embraced by many nations with legal and political traditions dramatically different from those of our own. This includes such states as Cambodia, Iran, Haiti, Nigeria, Sudan, Syria, and Yemen, all of which have been implicated in torture or extrajudicial killings or both.

Even our closest allies, including European states following the civil law system, begin with a very different assumption about the powers of courts and the rights of the accused. Nevertheless, if it is permitted to be established, the ICC will claim the power to try individual Americans, including U.S. service personnel and officials acting fully in accordance with U.S. law and our interests. The Court itself would be the final arbiter of its own power, and there would be no appeal from its decisions.

In 1791, Thomas Jefferson, our country's first Secretary of State, said:

"No court can have jurisdiction over a sovereign nation."

Last year this Congress prohibited the use of taxpayers' money to support the International Criminal Court. I say, let's put another lock on that door by adopting this amendment, the Craig amendment, and let's put a lock on the door to the Preparatory Commission as well.

In closing, I quote again from Mr. Jefferson. Thomas Jefferson said:

"It is the right of every nation to prohibit acts of sovereignty from being exercised by any other within its limits."

I urge my colleagues to join me in exercising this right and supporting this amendment to protect the sovereignty of the American people.

[Congressional Record: S9242-9243]

" This is not mere payback; it is an escalation in a bitter battle by the Senate Democrats to keep judges off this court who properly construe the Constitution and respect the laws duly enacted by the elected legislature. That is disappointing, and it is dangerous. The Senate Democrats' filibuster is a recipe for endless gridlock and a terrible disservice to the American people and the administration of justice. "

MIGUEL ESTRADA AND JUDICIAL OBSTRUCTION

February 10, 2003

M r. President, it is my pleasure to rise and speak on behalf of Miguel Estrada, a fellow Virginian and President Bush's nominee to serve on the U.S. Court of Appeals for the District of Columbia.

I have been listening to the Senator from New York and listening to his description of what is fair and reasonable. I do find it interesting that the Senator, on several occasions, talked about the standards of questions that were propounded in years past by Senator Ashcroft.

If Senator Ashcroft was such a wonderful model for questioning and judicial standards, I do find it interesting that that same Senator from New York, when given an opportunity to vote for Senator Ashcroft to be Attorney General, voted against him. So we do see some inconsistencies on citing Senator Ashcroft and then not voting for him.

Let's focus on this situation and the nomination before this body: Miguel Estrada. Miguel Estrada is a highly qualified nominee to be a judge. He has impeccable character. People always look at the character of an individual to determine how that person will act when put in a position of responsibility. One way to judge is by their past performance.

Some will say that Miguel Estrada does not have judicial experience. There are others who have been appointed to the courts who do not have judicial experience. So then you try to determine their judicial philosophy. I am convinced, in my examination of Miguel Estrada, that he has the right judicial philosophy. I am confident that when Miguel Estrada puts on that robe and is appointed for life, he will understand that judges are to interpret the law, not to make the law, which is the responsibility of the legislative branch. I am very confident that as a judge on the DC Court of Appeals, Miguel Estrada will adhere to this principle.

Others have said that since he has not been a judge, how are we going to know about his temperament. There are not many Latino or Hispanic Americans who serve on the federal courts. By arguing that he has not had judicial experience, and therefore, he cannot serve, implicitly would make it very difficult, if nearly impossible, for many Hispanic Americans to serve on the federal bench.

Miguel Estrada has justifiably been called the personification of the American dream. He was born in Honduras and immigrated to the United States when he was a teenager at the age of 17. He learned English as a second language and then went on and ultimately graduated with honors—magna cum laude from Columbia College and magna cum laude from Harvard Law School. He was even a member of the editorial board of the Harvard Law Review.

Mr. Estrada went on to serve as a law clerk on the U.S. Court of Appeals for the Second Circuit and also served as the Assistant to the Solicitor General of the United States. During his legal career, Miguel Estrada argued 15 cases in the Supreme Court of the United States, winning two-thirds of those cases.

Miguel Estrada has also performed significant pro bono service, or free legal services, including representation of a Virginia death row inmate before the U.S. Supreme Court, to which Miguel Estrada dedicated approximately 400 hours of time.

We previously heard from the Senator from New York that he wanted to determine whether Miguel Estrada had mainstream judicial values or had a mainstream view of the role of the courts in various cases, stare decisis, and precedent.

Miguel Estrada has unanimously earned the highest rating of "well qualified" from the American Bar Association. The American Bar Association's rating is based on "integrity, professional competence and judicial temperament."

In addition, Miguel Estrada's nomination is strongly supported by the Hispanic National Bar Association; the League of United Latin American Citizens, LULAC, which is the nation's oldest and largest Hispanic civil rights organization; the United States Hispanic Chamber of Commerce; and the Hispanic Business Roundtable.

Miguel Estrada is also supported by these other mainstream organizations: The Latino Coalition; the National Association for Small Disadvantaged Businesses; the Mexican American Grocers Association; the Hispanic Chambers of Commerce from a variety of towns and cities across the country, including the Greater Kansas City area and Las Cruces; the Puerto Rican American Foundations; the Federation of Mayors of Puerto Rico; the Hispanic Engineers Business Corporation; the Association for the Advancement of Mexican Americans; Nueva Esperanza; the Hispanic Engineers Business Corporation, the Hispanic Contractors of America, the Cuban Liberty Council, the Cuban American Voters National Community, and the Cuban American National Foundation.

This is a broad spectrum of individuals, organizations and associations from a variety of backgrounds and enterprises from all across the country which are very much a part of the mainstream of America which support Miguel Estrada.

I believe the Senate's prompt action on Mr. Estrada's long-delayed nomination is especially important. The DC Court of Appeals is one of the most important courts of appeal in the entire country, with cases of national implication. It is a primary forum for determining the legality of federal regulations and laws that control vast areas of American life. Recent retirements have left this court slowed down with four vacancies—four vacancies which are hindering the court's ability to decide cases expeditiously.

Delays in administration of justice in the DC Circuit Court of Appeals have consequences that can cost millions of dollars and affect thousands of lives. Indeed, justice delayed is justice denied.

The senior Senator from Massachusetts, Mr. Kennedy, said on this floor, at approximately 2:37 p.m., that he was concerned about the process of the Miguel Estrada nomination. I will express my concerns about the process.

Today there is a crisis in our courts, as too many federal courts lack a sufficient number of judges, especially the DC Court of Appeals, which has four of their 12 judgeships vacant. That means 33 percent of the DC Court of Appeals has vacancies in those seats.

What Senator Hatch and I want is fair consideration and confirmation of the President's well-qualified and diverse judicial nominees. While many on the other side may work to hijack the nominations process to score partisan political points or obstruct fair consideration, this nomination deserves a vote. It has deserved a vote for a long time.

This nomination has been pending since May 9, 2001. That is over 20 months ago. A hearing was not even held for Miguel Estrada until September of 2002.

I respectfully urge my colleagues to fill these vacancies—particularly this vacancy on the DC Circuit Court—and vote to confirm Miguel Estrada.

Look at the record. You will find that Miguel Estrada is superbly qualified to serve on the DC Circuit. Indeed, Miguel Estrada is an American success story, with exemplary credentials and qualifications. Hispanic Americans will rejoice in his success, as indeed all Americans will rejoice and applaud his success.

I join my Latino constituents in saying: Sigamos adelante con Miguel Estrada. Let us move forward with Miguel Estrada.

[Congressional Record: S2107-2108]

March 4, 2003

Mr. President, I rise once again to support Miguel Estrada's nomination to serve on the United States Court of Appeals for the District of Columbia. Miguel Estrada is being treated unfairly by Senators on the other side of the aisle who continue to practice such blatant obstructionism in an effort to score petty partisan points. Indeed, the obstructing Senators are shirking, in my view, their duty by avoiding a vote on this gentleman, Miguel Estrada, who was nominated 22 months ago by President Bush.

This is not mere payback; it is an escalation in a bitter battle by the Senate Democrats to keep judges off this court who properly construe the Constitution and respect the laws duly enacted by the elected legislature. That is disappointing, and it is dangerous.

The Senate Democrats' filibuster is a recipe for endless gridlock and a terrible disservice to the American people and the administration of justice.

Our protracted debate on the nomination of Miguel Estrada to the Court of Appeals for the District of Columbia makes clear the importance of sound reasoning judges on our circuit courts. For example, look at the recent denial of a rehearing decision by another circuit court, the Ninth Circuit Court of Appeals. I object to the decision by the Ninth Circuit Court of Appeals which will strip the Pledge of Allegiance from classrooms and over 9,600,000 students in Western United States. This decision is a miscarriage of justice.

The majority opinion lacks a clear reading of the constitutional intent and the legal precedent, and there is clearly a lack of common sense. This decision, frankly, is an abuse of power by the majority of those judges who sit on the Ninth Circuit Court of Appeals.

We all know well the history of our Nation and the fundamental ideas of freedom, particularly those of religious freedom, which in Virginia we call the first freedom. It was because of the desire to worship freely, to escape religious persecution in European countries that many came to settle in the American Colonies, from Pilgrims to French Huguenots. From New England to Virginia to South Carolina, many came to settle in this country to get away from Europe, ruled in large part by monarchs who served not by any talent, quality, or the consent of the people, but, as they called it, divine right. That divine right was generally conferred upon them by the exclusive monopoly of one church. So there was a co-conspiracy of a monarchy and an exclusive religion.

In the Virginia Colony, it was the Anglican Church that was forced upon the people. Baptists, in particular, were forced to pay to that established church. Indeed, when they talk about the Danbury letter to the Baptists, the Baptists were very happy when Thomas Jefferson was elected President. If one looks at what is in the Virginia statute of religious freedom, which was the predecessor of part of the first amendment of the Bill of Rights in the U.S. Constitution, one gets a better sense of what religious freedom and the so-called establishment clause is all about.

I will read from article I, section 16, in the Virginia Constitution that still remains and, of course, is built upon Mr. Jefferson's statute of religious freedom which was also involved in the Virginia Declaration of Rights which became eventually the first amendment to the Constitution.

It reads:

"That religion or the duty which we owe to our Creator, and the manner of discharging it, can be directed only by reason and conviction, not by force or violence; and, therefore, all men are equally entitled to the free exercise of religion, according to the dictates of conscience; and that it is the mutual duty of all to practice Christian forbearance, love, and charity towards each other. No man shall be compelled to frequent or support any religious worship, place, or ministry whatsoever, nor shall be enforced, restrained, molested, or burthened in his body or goods, nor shall otherwise suffer on account of his religious opinions or belief; but all men shall be free to profess and by argument to maintain their opinions in matters of religion, and the same shall in nowise diminish, enlarge, or affect their civil capacities. And the General Assembly shall not prescribe any religious test whatever, or confer any peculiar privileges or advantages on any sect or denomination, or pass any law requiring or authorizing any religious society, or the people of any district within this Commonwealth, to levy on themselves or others, any tax for the erection or repair of any house of public worship, or for the support of any church or ministry; but it shall be left free to every person to select his religious instructor, and to make for his support such private contract as he shall please."

That, in my view, is the full historical context, from the founding documents since Virginia first passed the Statute of Religious Freedom, of what the first amendment should be.

Obviously, the first amendment of our Constitution is but a few sentences, but this gives the historical and the legal grounding of the Statute of Religious Freedom.

We all know well the words written by Thomas Jefferson proclaiming our independence from the religiously oppressive British monarchy. These words allowed our young Nation to:

"Assume the powers of the Earth, the separate and equal station to which laws of nature and of nature's God."

These are words that tell all of us, as Americans, that all men are endowed by their Creator with certain unalienable rights, that among these are life, liberty, and the pursuit of happiness. These words still stir our hearts. They inspire us to continue to build that shining city on a hill, to be that beacon of freedom, religious or otherwise, for people all around the world.

Our Constitution, the hallowed document, can be summed up by one word and one idea: Freedom. The Constitution and the institution and the formation of this Government to protect those God-given rights and those freedoms states that Congress shall make no law respecting the establishment of religion.

While some conveniently use this to perpetrate actions such as those we saw out in San Francisco last week, it is often forgotten that the Constitution just as clearly states that the Congress shall make no law prohibiting the free exercise thereof.

I feel confident that the scholarly Miguel Estrada, who was editor of the Harvard Law Review, would have views similar to the dissent written by Judges O'Scannlain and Ferdinand Fernandez. As Judge O'Scannlain notes in his well-reasoned and thoughtful dissent, this decision of the Ninth Circuit Court is wrong on many levels. It is wrong because reciting of the Pledge of Allegiance is simply not a religious act, as the two-judge majority asserts. The decision is wrong as a matter of Supreme Court precedent as properly understood. The decision is wrong because it denies the will of the people of California as expressed in section 52720 of the California education code, and it is wrong as a matter of common sense.

I trust the Supreme Court of the United States will grant a writ of certiorari and promptly hear and decide this case. I, of course, hope they will reverse it. Parenthetically, I support the resolution of Senator Lisa Murkowski of Alaska expressing support for the Pledge of Allegiance, and I ask unanimous consent that I be added as a cosponsor of that measure. ...

In the realm of public education, the Supreme Court—and the Presiding Officer of the Senate right now is well aware of precedent in the various decisions the Supreme Court has made when dealing in the realm and the issue of public education and prayer, or the religious tests. There are at least three different but interrelated tests used to analyze alleged violations of the establishment clause—in other words, the establishment of a religion. It is a three-pronged test, first articulated in the case of *Lemon v. Kurtzman*, called the Lemon test, and that is to determine whether that public activity had a primarily secular purpose. Here, the Pledge of Allegiance is primarily a patriotic event and purpose.

The second test is called the endorsement test. Here, there is no endorsement of any denomination of any religion. So that test is passed.

The third test is called the coercion test, and there is no coercion here for students.

The Supreme Court of the United States has commented that the presence of "one nation under God" in the Pledge of Allegiance is constitutional. The Supreme Court will have an opportunity to clearly resolve this because sometimes there are judges who have to be reversed on many occasions before they understand the plain intent of the law, of previous opinions and the history of our country.

I will not discuss how the Ninth Circuit erred in the applications of the facts of this case to the establishment clause, but I do commend to my colleagues the dissent of Judge O'Scannlain, which I hope will give guidance to the Justices of the U.S. Supreme Court when they do review this case.

As a resource, I direct the attention of my colleagues to some outstanding historical analysis prepared by a gentleman from Texas, David Barton, and an organization called Wall Builders.

If reciting the pledge is truly a religious act, in violation of the establishment clause, then so the recitation of our Constitution itself would be, which refers to the "year of our Lord" and our Declaration of Independence, which contains multiple references to God. Our Founders claimed the right to dissolve the political bands based on the laws of nature and of nature's God.

The most famous passage, of course, is the "all men are created equal" and they are "endowed by their Creator with certain unalienable rights."

Subsequently, the signatories "appeal to the Supreme Judge of the world to rectify their intentions"; our national motto, which is "in God we trust"; and the singing of the national anthem, a verse which says: "And this motto: In God we trust."

Furthermore, the Supreme Court, even the Ninth Circuit Court of Appeals, opens sessions with a call that says, "God save the United States and this honorable court."

There is an undeniable and historical relationship between God and our Founders and the Government leaders throughout our history. In fact, it was Congress in 1837, acting on the will of the people, that authorized the motto "In God We Trust" to be printed on our currency. We can cite the actions of the entire body of Founding Fathers. For example, in 1800 when Washington, DC, became the Nation's Capital and the President moved to the White House and Congress into the Capitol, Congress approved the use of the Capitol Building as a church building for Christian worship services. In fact, Christian worship services on Sunday were started at the Treasury Building and at the War Office.

A scant review of the legislative history in States and the Federal Government and the intent of our Founders, from George Washington to Thomas Jefferson, lays out the utter absurdity—no; actually, the arrogance—of this Ninth Circuit Court of Appeals and this decision.

Each of us who has the high privilege to sit in this Chamber is very well aware of the circumstances by which the phrase "one nation under God" became a part of the pledge in 1954. It was the will of the Congress, the will of the people, that put it there, and today it is a will, unfortunately, of a few unelected judges who seek to remove it.

The State of California is not unique in encouraging students to engage in appropriate patriotic exercise. My Commonwealth of Virginia has a statute requiring the daily recitation of the Pledge of Allegiance in every classroom. It is thoughtfully crafted. The Virginia statute provides that:

"No student shall be compelled to recite the Pledge if he, his parent or legal guardian, objects on religious, philosophical or other grounds to his participating in this exercise. Students who are thus exempt from reciting the Pledge shall remain quietly standing or sitting at their desk while others recite the Pledge. ..."

As Governor of the Commonwealth of Virginia, I was proud to have been able to sign into law a commonsense provision to develop guidelines for reciting the Pledge of Allegiance in public schools in 1996.

While we can go on about this, the point is that the pledge is a patriotic exercise. Thomas Jefferson, who authored the Statute of Religious Freedom, had no intention of allowing the Government to limit, restrict, regulate, or interfere with public religious practices. He believed, along with the other Founders, that the first amendment had been enacted only to prevent the Federal establishment of a national denomination. This patriotic pledge establishes no religious denomination.

These Ninth Circuit Court judges discredit, in my view, the judiciary. This is an example of government overreach in a very different and harmful way. It is judicial activism at its very worst. It is activism by unelected judges who, through this decision, and decisions such as this, usurp the policymaking role given to this body and to the people of the States, the rights that are guaranteed to all of us and the people in the States by the U.S. Constitution.

Let me take a moment to put this decision into context.

The Ninth Circuit Court of Appeals has a long recent record of issuing decisions that are clearly out of step with most Americans—I daresay, reality—and out of the bounds of American jurisprudence.

The court has become famous—maybe I should say infamous—for several decisions. The Ninth Circuit Court is the most overturned appeals court in the country. The decisions issued by this court have been reversed by the U.S. Supreme Court more frequently and by a larger margin than any other court of appeals in the Nation. In recent years, the reversal rate has hovered around 80 percent.

In one recent session of the Supreme Court alone, an astonishing 28 out of 29 appeal decisions of the Ninth Circuit Court of Appeals were overturned—97 percent were overturned.

What is the next decision out of this Ninth Circuit Court of Appeals? Will they ban the singing of "God Bless America" in our schools? Will they redact our founding documents, some of which are the greatest documents in all the history of mankind and civilization? Will the Congress, the Supreme Court, and State legislatures across the land be prohibited from opening their sessions by saying the pledge because that somehow might offend the sensibilities of someone watching a legislative body open with the Pledge of Allegiance?

The fact is, this is not an argument of God or no God. It is not an argument about separation of church and state. It is not an argument of the establishment of a religious denomination. Saying the pledge is no more a religious act than is purchasing a candy bar with a coin that says "In God We Trust."

Let us understand the fact is this, and I think most Americans agree: The Pledge of Allegiance should remain in our schools and other public functions. As it is today, it should be a voluntary matter of personal conscience. On this issue and so many others, the Ninth Circuit Court of Appeals is out of touch and flat out wrong. This errant decision clearly points out the need to put commonsense, reasonable, well-grounded judges on the Federal bench, rather than dangerous activists who ignore the will of the people of the States, who ignore common sense, and apparently disagree with or are pitifully ignorant of the foundational principles of these United States.

This is a wake-up call, a wake-up call for those on the other side of the aisle who are holding up the confirmation of people like Miguel Estrada, while at the same time maybe signing on to Senator Murkowski's resolution or maybe at the same time coming down to the floor to rail against activist decisions such as the one that came out of the Ninth Circuit last week.

I have come to this floor many times, as I know the Presiding Officer has, to advocate for Mr. Estrada. The fact is, he is qualified. He has earned the unanimous highest rating from the American Bar Association, the rating that my friends on the other side of the aisle have previously, on other nominees, described as a gold standard for judicial nominees.

Mr. Estrada embodies the modern-day American dream that we so fondly talk about. He, like many others who came to this country in recent decades, came from a Latin American country. He, like those who came to Jamestown, VA, in 1607, or in a later year, Cajuns, Irish, Scottish, German, Scandinavian, Italian, Polish, Korean, Vietnamese, Pakistani, Indian, Lebanese, Persians, or even my own mother, all came to this country to seek out a better life. He has overcome tremendous obstacles. He has worked hard. He has embraced the opportunity that became available to better himself and found a fulfilling life in this land of opportunity.

Now Miguel Estrada stands at the precipice of service on an important DC Court of Appeals. He is ready, qualified, and more than able to take the next step, and for no other reason than scoring political points his nomination is being obstructed, delayed, and denied.

Let me say very clearly, those who deny Mr. Estrada a vote by this body are doing more harm than they realize. For Miguel Estrada and every other person who believes the American dream can happen, that shining city on the hill is dimmed today because of the partisan games taking place in this body. I respectfully encourage those on the other side of the aisle to take a lesson today. Do the right thing. Work your will and constitutional responsibilities. Have the gumption to take a stand and cast your vote.

I have no problem in taking a stand in explaining why I support Miguel Estrada. For those who are opposed, have the gumption to vote no and then explain your vote rather than perpetrating this irresponsible, duplicitous filibuster, which is thwarting the will of the majority of the Senators.

Concerning both the Pledge of Allegiance and the confirmation of Miguel Estrada, the power of the dream and the promise of America is rooted in one idea: that the direction of our Nation is and will always be determined by the consent and will of the people. The consent and will of the people is not being effectuated by the irresponsibility of a few, whether they be judges on the Ninth Circuit Court of Appeals or the Senate. Senators need to exercise their responsibilities to advise and consent on nominees.

I hope and pray the U.S. Supreme Court will reverse this egregious decision to ban the Pledge of Allegiance in the Western States of our country. I also hope and pray that Senators will exercise their duty, take a stand, vote yes or no, explain it to their constituents, and the will and the consent of the majority of the people of this country will be effectuated.

I close by saying, God bless America.

[Congressional Record: S3054-3057]

"I am proud today, only days before the 226th anniversary of our Nation's birth, of our Declaration of Independence, where we ceded from the monarchy of Britain, that we are going to stand for what is right. We are going to stand by our flag and the principles of freedom and justice and with our Pledge of Allegiance."

"Under God" in Pledge

June 26, 2002

M adam President, I associate myself with the remarks of the
Senator from Louisiana, Ms. Landrieu, and I commend her for
her resolution. With her consent, I would like to add my name to her resolution in the event the Ninth Circuit and the Supreme Court continue this
errant miscarriage of justice.

Madam President, we often talk about miscarriages of justice, but today
I talk about an instance in which proper administration of justice was
dragged into a dark alley and mugged.

Many of us are outraged to learn today that a divided three-judge panel
of the Ninth Circuit Court of Appeals believed it knew better than the properly exercised wisdom of the people and their duly elected representatives in
striking down the Pledge of Allegiance and stating that the Pledge of
Allegiance is unconstitutional. These judges ignored the very basis of our
democracy and representative Government. They have ignored, right before
Independence Day, the spirit of our country that Mr. Jefferson, in the

Declaration of Independence, proclaimed to the British monarchy, which had an established religion, that our rights are God-given rights.

He stated in the Declaration of Independence that we are endowed by our Creator "with certain unalienable Rights, that among these are Life, Liberty and the pursuit of Happiness." All of this came from the Virginia Declaration of Rights which expressed the same sentiments.

Let's understand, if these judges do not understand, with their judicial activist decisions such as this, the judges are to interpret the laws, they are not to write the laws. The laws on the Pledge of Allegiance and the laws for the recitation of the Pledge of Allegiance in our schools are passed by State legislatures all across our country. They are reflecting the will, the desire, and the value of the people in their States and in their communities.

Let's also understand that these activist judges, like the two involved in this majority decision of the Ninth Circuit, often cite the first 10 words of the Establishment Clause, which says:

"Congress shall make no law respecting an establishment of religion..."

But they too often forget the six words that follow:

"...or prohibiting the free exercise thereof."

To understand the history of religious freedom in this country, one must understand that this country, in the very beginning, starting with the Virginia Company, which was a commercial venture—it still was a crown colony, as were all the colonies, and as such it was associated with the Church of England or the Anglican Church. People were compelled to pay taxes to that church whether they wanted to go to that church or not.

The concept of the statute of religious freedom first started in Virginia with Thomas Jefferson. He drafted the Virginia Statute for Religious Freedom. It is on his gravestone as one of his three most proud accomplishments, along with the founding of the University of Virginia, and drafting the Declaration of Independence.

The statute of religious freedom was a novel idea. It was a radical idea because what you had in the 1700s and before then were monarchies, theocracies in effect, where the monarchs were ruling because of bloodlines not because of merit or popular will. They also had a single church and that church was given that exclusive monopoly in that they would then say that those monarchs were ruling by divine guidance and divine right. In all of these monarchies, the idea that people could believe as they saw fit and not be compelled to join a church or be compelled to support a church was a very radical idea and upsetting to the tyrannical monarchs because that upset their whole justification for being in power in the first place.

The Virginia Statute for Religious Freedom actually took 7 years to pass in the Virginia General Assembly. Good ideas still sometimes take a long time. Mr. Jefferson was the Minister to France when James Madison finally got this Statute through the Virginia General Assembly.

The Virginia Statute for Religious Freedom states very clearly, in article I, section 16, of the Virginia Constitution, "That religion, or the duty which we owe our Creator and the manner of discharging it, can be directed by reason and conviction, not by force or violence; and therefore, all men are equally entitled to the free exercise of religion, according to the dictates of conscience; …" and so forth. It goes on to say that people's rights and individual's rights should not be enhanced nor should they be diminished due to their religious beliefs.

Now the purpose of the Establishment Clause, which was then put into the Federal Constitution in the First Amendment of the Bill of Rights, was not to expunge religion or matters of faith from all aspects of public life. The Pledge of Allegiance should remain in our schools and other public functions, but it should be voluntary. The Commonwealth of Virginia has such a law but it is voluntary. If a student does not want to recite the Pledge of Allegiance, he or she is not compelled to do so. One needs to respect that individual conscience.

The way it is in the law, whether in this case in the Ninth Circuit or elsewhere, is that it allows, in accordance with the founding documents of our Nation, the ability of the majority to express their values and their wisdom. If somebody somehow does not want to recite it, they are not compelled to do so.

So the Establishment Clause, as well as our Bill of Rights, and our Declaration of Independence, are all modeled on the Virginia Statute for Religious Freedom, and the Virginia Declaration of Rights.

The Virginia Statute for Religious Freedom, as drafted by Mr. Jefferson and then carried forward by James Madison and adopted in 1786, counsels against the impious presumption of legislators and rulers, civil as well as ecclesiastical, who being themselves but fallible and uninspired men who have assumed dominion over the faith of others.

The Virginia Declaration of Rights holds that all men are equally entitled to the free exercise of religion according to the dictates of their conscience. Minimal reference is made to a nondenominational creator or natural rights or God and that is consistent with the values and the desires of the people. This is in step, and the laws are, fortunately, in this regard, in step with our society and the views of the people, as they have been throughout our history.

It is my hope, and it is not without basis, that this decision of the Ninth Circuit will be handily reversed by the Supreme Court of the United States.

I remind the Senate that the Ninth Circuit Court of Appeals has by far the most dismal reversal rate in the Supreme Court of any court of appeals in our land. In recent years, the reversal rate has hovered around 80 percent compared to about 50 percent for the next highest circuit, which is the Eighth Circuit. In one recent session of the Supreme Court alone, an astonishing 28 out of 29 decisions of the Ninth Circuit Court were overturned. That is 97 percent. What ruling from the Ninth Circuit will come next? Are they going to white out passages of the Declaration of Independence? Will it be improper to recite on public grounds the Declaration of Independence because it refers to our Creator giving us unalienable rights? Will the Ninth Circuit order currency and our coinage to knock out the insidious message of "In God We Trust"? Will they say that all coins have to be destroyed and melted down? Will they imprison school choirs and have the school directors imprisoned because the children are singing "God Bless America"? Who knows what is next out of the Ninth Circuit.

At some point, though, a proper respect for the rights of the people, their desires, and also common sense and reason must be guiding our courts, especially this particular circuit court, and today's activist, offensive decision.

Today's action by the Ninth Circuit is hit-and-run jurisprudence. It is smug judicial activism at its rankest. It is outrageously out-of-touch with the desires and values of the American people. It is striking down the basic concept that laws made by Congress or by State legislatures, unless they are clearly unconstitutional, ought to be respected.

I am proud today, only days before the 226th anniversary of our Nation's birth, of our Declaration of Independence, where we ceded from the monarchy of Britain, that we are going to stand for what is right. We are going to stand by our flag and the principles of freedom and justice and with our Pledge of Allegiance.

I thank my colleagues for their united, bipartisan stand for what is right about America and what is right for our schools and our youngsters, and that is stating the Pledge of Allegiance to our flag.

[Congressional Record: S6108-6109]

" Under this bill, if an unborn child is injured or killed during the commission of an already-defined Federal crime of violence, then the assailant could be charged with a separate offense for the second, enhanced crime upon the unborn child. "

UNBORN VICTIMS OF VIOLENCE

March 25, 2004

Mr. President, I rise today in support of the Unborn Victims of Violence Act, or what many individuals refer to as "Laci and Conner's Law."

We have all heard the tragic story of Laci and Conner Peterson; Laci, 8 months pregnant with her unborn son Conner, were viciously murdered at the hands of a killer. Regrettably, Laci and Conner's story is only one of many instances where a woman is harmed and may not only lose her life but the life of her unborn child.

In my Commonwealth of Virginia, we had a similar tragic situation occur in April of 2002. Ronda Robinson was maliciously gunned down in her Lynchburg home, while her two daughters watched in terror. Like Laci, Ronda was in her third trimester when she and her unborn child had their lives taken.

At that time, Virginia did not have a fetal homicide law on the books, and the Commonwealth was unable to bring a homicide charge against the murderer for the killing of Ronda's unborn child.

Unfortunately, the situation in Virginia and many other States remains the same. If a mother survives an assault, but loses her unborn child, the law currently does not recognize any loss of any human life at all.

However, I am pleased that the Virginia General Assembly has taken steps to correct this wrong. This year, the Virginia General Assembly overwhelmingly passed legislation that would hold an individual accountable who, "unlawfully, willfully, deliberately, maliciously, and with premeditation kills the fetus of another." Twenty-Nine senators or 72 percent of the Senate and 77 members of the House of Delegates or 77 percent of the house supported this legislation.

While this legislation has not yet been signed into law, I am hopeful that Virginia will follow the lead of the 29 other States that have passed this important and meaningful legislation.

I have the same optimism for the Unborn Victims of Violence Act. We have a chance to hear the voice of the voiceless and bring fairness to a system that has essentially told hundreds of women and their families, their unborn child never existed.

I have been blessed with four great gifts, my loving wife and my three wonderful children. I have witnessed my children grow and live healthy and happy lives. I see what my children have accomplished so far in their lives and I am eager to see what other great accomplishments will follow. But many individuals are unable to witness the birth and growth of their child because of a violent criminal act.

Throughout my tenure in public service, whether it was in the Virginia House of Delegates, U.S. House of Representatives, Governor's office, or now in the U.S. Senate, I have always tried to be tough on criminals. I have always believed in the principle that if you commit a crime, you should be punished.

The Unborn Victims of Violence Act closely upholds my beliefs by making criminals accountable for their actions. Under current Federal law, an individual who commits a Federal crime of violence and kills or injures an unborn child cannot be prosecuted for those violent acts against the unborn child. The Unborn Victims of Violence Act seeks to rectify this situation and close that loophole.

Under this bill, if an unborn child is injured or killed during the commission of an already-defined Federal crime of violence, then the assailant could be charged with a separate offense for the second, enhanced crime upon the unborn child.

Opponents of the Unborn Victims of Violence Act contend that this will hamper a woman's right to choose and constitute an attack on Roe v. Wade. This is simply false. In fact, this legislation explicitly provides that it does not apply to any abortion to which a woman has consented, to any act of the mother herself, legal or illegal, or to any form of medical treatment.

In addition, opponents have brought numerous challenges against State unborn victims laws, based on Roe and other constitutional arguments, and all of these challenges have been rejected by State and Federal courts.

I have always been a strong supporter of rights of the people in the States to determine their laws so long as it does not harm interstate commerce or our Constitution. This bill safeguards those States' laws. This legislation does not supersede State unborn victims laws, nor does it impose such a law in a State that does not have one on the books. The Unborn Victims of Violence Act merely applies to an already defined set of Federal crimes.

The bottom line is that criminals must be held accountable for their actions. The Unborn Victims of Violence Act ensures that justice is sought and available for the totality of the violent murderous act. This is good, solid legislation that is tough on crime, appropriately punishes criminals, and meets the ends of justice desired by law-abiding citizens.

I urge my colleagues to support this bill so that we can send it to President Bush for his signature and ensure that justice will be served.

[Congressional Record: S3165-3166]

" It is Ronald Reagan's inspiring character, courage, unflinching adherence to principles, policies, and eloquence that brought forth a renaissance for the United States of America, a rebirth of freedom, and the world also experienced that renaissance at a crucial juncture in history. He fanned the flames of freedom and that torch of liberty will continue to burn brightly by his inspiration and example. We all thank God for blessing the United States and the world with Ronald Reagan. "

TRIBUTE TO RONALD REAGAN

June 8, 2004

M r. President, my colleagues and Americans, President Ronald Reagan will be returning to Washington tomorrow for the very last time. I rise to honor the memory and life of the greatest leader of the 20th century and to express my sympathy to his wonderful and loyal family—in particular, his loving wife and partner Nancy.

Nancy Reagan has always been an outstanding and inspirational role model for our entire Nation. And that has never been more clearly displayed than through her wonderful courage and love during the difficult journey she and President Reagan traveled during the past decade.

Like so many, I was inspired to actually answer the call of public service because of then-Governor Ronald Reagan's positive, principled message. In 1976, I began as a young lieutenant in the Reagan revolution when I was asked to chair Young Virginians for Reagan. Today, I am still motivated to work to advance his individual-empowering philosophy in government.

Ronald Reagan entered the political stage in 1964 with a speech which summed up a philosophy that would guide him through his Presidency two decades hence, and which turned the tide of world history.

Mr. Reagan said in 1964, "You and I have a rendezvous with destiny. We can preserve for our children this, the last best hope of man on Earth, or we can sentence them to take the first step into a thousand years of darkness. If we fail, at least let our children say of us we justified our brief moment here. We did all that could be done."

Indeed, Ronald Wilson Reagan did have a rendezvous with destiny. President Reagan rejuvenated the spirit of America. His determined, optimistic leadership lit the torch of liberty and allowed it to shine in the dark recesses of oppressed countries around the world.

Ronald Reagan believed in the innate goodness of mankind. He believed and advocated the wisdom of our country's foundational principles. He believed that given the opportunity, all men and women would seek freedom and liberty and with it unleash creativity, ingenuity, hard work, and economic growth.

He touched deeply the hearts and minds of Americans through his genuinely believed, commonsense conservative words of encouragement— from his first inaugural speech in 1981, to his inspirational State of the Union Addresses, to his moving memorial tribute to our lost Challenger explorer, to his strong demand to tear down the wall of oppression, to his passionate tribute to the defenders of liberty at Normandy 20 years ago this week. Those were the words he delivered. Those words which he delivered are now as much a part of the fabric of America as the threads of our flag, Old Glory. Lee Greenwood's song, "God Bless the U.S.A.," was an anthem to Ronald Reagan's renewed America.

Historians will surely discuss and debate the impact of Ronald Reagan's 8 years as President for generations to come. But there is no doubt his legacy has already been revealed. In fact, he foresaw his legacy. He was there at the bicentennial in 1981 of the Battle of Yorktown. He gave a wonderful speech at Yorktown, VA.

He said as follows, "We have come to this field to celebrate the triumph of an idea—that freedom will eventually triumph over tyranny. It is and always will be a warning to those who would usurp the rights of others. Time will find them beaten. The beacon of freedom shines here for all who will see, inspiring free men and captives alike, and no wall, no curtain, nor totalitarian state can shut it out."

To put this in context, when Ronald Reagan became our 40th President, Americans had lost their faith in our leaders and in the role of America in the world. Government at home was restraining its citizens with oppressive taxation and burdensome regulations. Our national malaise led to historically high unemployment, high interest rates and inflation, low productivity, and a stagnant stock market.

Our moral authority around the world had been eroding, and confidence in the ideals of liberty and democracy were replaced by the fear of expanding tyranny, communism, and repression.

America yearned for a leader who could change the direction of our Nation and make them proud of our heritage once again. Ronald Reagan answered that call.

Many tributes this week rightfully point to President Reagan's unwavering optimism and belief in the inner strength of Americans, and indeed all human beings. He understood that they could be motivated and inspired to higher ideals with our competitive nature.

No more hand-wringing. He wanted action. Indeed, he challenged us to look no further than his administration and ourselves for solutions. He said, "If not us, who? If not now, when?"

Beyond his unshakable faith in mankind was his consistent adherence to principles which were unfashionable and often scorned when he came to office but today which are solidly embraced and winning the minds of people across our country and throughout the world. He acted on his beliefs that government interference should be restrained and that free people should be unrestrained, without limits. We prospered and we thrived with the creation of jobs and opportunities.

One of my very favorite principles of President Reagan was declared in his 1985 State of the Union address when he said, "Every dollar the government does not take from us, every decision it does not make for us, will make our economy stronger, our lives more abundant and our future more free."

And so it is. Through tax cuts that return tax dollars to those whose hard work and ingenuity earned them, to reducing burdensome regulations, President Reagan presided over the beginning of the most robust peace expansion of our economy in the history of our Nation.

But President Reagan believed the blessings of liberty must not be bestowed only on a few nations and only to those blessed to be born on free soil; Ronald Reagan, with the strength of his convictions, exported and advanced democracy to continents, countries, and people yearning to taste the sweet nectar of liberty.

He knew the evil communistic empire could not be sustained and would collapse under the weight of a determined effort to challenge the Soviets on their failed policies, both foreign and domestic. He reversed decades of policy calling for containment of that oppressive tyrannical system, and he boldly asserted that the advancement of freedom and liberty must be America's No. 1 foreign policy objective. Indeed, he believed that it is our solemn moral obligation to do so.

Now we are seeing his greatest legacy. Hundreds of millions of free people, from the Baltics in Lithuania, Estonia, Latvia through Poland, Hungary, Slovenia, Slovakia, the Czech Republic, Bulgaria and Romania, all people once repressed behind the Iron Curtain are now joining NATO. They are true friends and allies. Yes, they are breathing that invigorating wind of freedom.

One of the last public statements Ronald Reagan made was in 1983. He provided us with a vision which will guide us now and in the future. Ronald Reagan said, "History comes and history goes, but principles endure and ensure future generations to defend liberty—not as a gift from the government, but a blessing from our Creator. Here in America the lamp of individual conscience burns bright. By that I know we will all be guided to that dreamed of day when no one wields a sword and no one drags a chain."

It is Ronald Reagan's inspiring character, courage, unflinching adherence to principles, policies, and eloquence that brought forth a renaissance for the United States of America, a rebirth of freedom, and the world also experienced that renaissance at a crucial juncture in history. He fanned the flames of freedom and that torch of liberty will continue to burn brightly by his inspiration and example. We all thank God for blessing the United States and the world with Ronald Reagan.

President Reagan, as you finally enter the gates of that shining city on the hill you always talked about, rest peacefully, knowing you left the world a much better place than it was when you arrived. For that, the free people of your Nation are eternally grateful.

[Congressional Record: S6605-6606]

February 3, 2005

Mr. President, I rise to speak about an American success story. It is one that ended, at least his life on Earth, in June of last year. It is to the story of a man who rose from humble beginnings and surroundings to become a leader. In fact, he became one of, if not the greatest leaders, in the 20th century, and I am talking about President Ronald Reagan.

This coming Sunday, February 6, would have been President Reagan's 94th birthday. I hope this weekend, when so many people in America will be watching the Super Bowl and all the festivities surrounding it, they will take a moment to remember not only Ronald Reagan's birth but to reflect on the positive impacts his life has had on so many people in America and around the world.

He was a man who stood strong for enduring foundational principles in the face of conflict and adversity at home and who faced down the Communist menace abroad. Through it all, he never lost touch with the decency and the morality of America that we aspire for in our leaders and indeed all of our citizens.

A few weeks ago, I took what I called a Ronald Reagan pilgrimage with my wife Susan and our three young kids to southern California. We went to the gravesite of the Reagan Presidential Library. There is also a museum, which is wonderful, and tells his whole life story.

We also trekked up through all the rains and floods and fog, up to Rancho del Cielo, the Reagan ranch. There, at that ranch, you see the core of Ronald Reagan, the substance of him. He spent 1 out of 8 days as President up at this ranch, which is 600 acres. It is a very humble place—small, as far as the housing. It had a small shower. He must have been elbowing that shower all the time, trying to take a shower there. That is where he rode his horses, cut wood, trimmed trees. You could see this is how Ronald Reagan kept his common sense. This is where you see the essence of the man, why he was so well grounded so that he could somehow see the future and keep the inspiration and appreciation of the grandeur of God's creation with the beauty of the trees and the rocks and mountains and the animals, but also recognizing what is great about this country, and the hard work and the personal strength it takes to do various things.

Ronald Reagan was a modern-day hero who embodied all that was great about George Washington and the spirits enunciated by Thomas Jefferson. His perseverance, his strength, his commitment to principle are lessons that taught me and taught many others. He was the person who inspired me and many others to get involved in organized politics and into public service. Today, thanks to Ronald Reagan, as I saw Ambassadors on the House floor from Lithuania, from Romania, throughout Central Europe—those were hundreds of millions of people who were behind the Iron Curtain. But, thanks to Ronald Reagan's perseverance, for his belief in the dignity of all human beings, that all people do yearn to be free, to exercise their God-given rights, those people who were behind that Iron Curtain, who were enemies, are now tasting that sweet nectar of liberty. They are our friends. They are our allies in this war on terror. Their numbers are growing, with greater hope and prosperity. Ronald Reagan helped make sure this century is the century of liberty.

While President Reagan's life here on Earth is over, his legacy continues to endure, motivate, and inspire me and others here in America and around the world. I hope on this weekend we will think of Nancy Reagan, say a prayer for her, remember and also thank God for one of the greatest blessings He has provided to us and that is the birth of Ronald Wilson Reagan.

[Congressional Record: S964-965]

"The seven aspirant countries have had to overcome significant political and economic difficulties to reach the precipice of NATO membership. Transforming a socialist-focused economy to one that is market based requires tremendous perseverance and visionary leadership and also an appreciation of liberty on the part of the people of these countries."

NATO

May 7, 2003

T hank you, Madam President. I thank the chairman of the Foreign Relations Committee, Senator Lugar, for his outstanding leadership on this issue. I also very much agree with the remarks made by Senator Hutchison of Texas.

As far as an enlarged NATO, we have had hearings on the mending of fences and the moving forward that we will need to have as a country with our Allies with a new sense of realism insofar as NATO and certain alliances—who we can always count on and who we sometimes may not be able to count on in the future.

I rise today to specifically address the issue of the enlargement of NATO. I offer my very strong support for the enlargement of the North Atlantic Treaty Organization alliance. The NATO alliance, over the decades, has had a positive impact on the world.

Since the days I was Governor of Virginia, I have been a long-time advocate of enlarging NATO, with new countries to contribute to security and also to advance individual liberty.

I was an advocate of admitting Poland, the Czech Republic, and

Hungary, and they have been good participatory members. You can see how the advancement of liberty has allowed the people of those countries to have greater freedoms and greater prosperity.

I believe that enlarging the alliance will bring even greater peace and security to the world, as well as confirm the value of economic reforms that will offer all people greater individual freedoms and protection of their rights.

The reforms and progress that have been made by Estonia, Latvia, Lithuania, Slovakia, Slovenia, Bulgaria, and Romania have transformed once communist, oppressive states into vibrant democracies that appreciate the newly reborn freedom to control their own destinies.

These nations are ascending into NATO at a serious time for the NATO alliance. As these countries have made a positive transformation, so must NATO transform from the cold war deterrent it has so successfully been over the last 50 years into an alliance that is able to adapt to meet the new challenges facing the world and the partner nations of NATO.

NATO and its members must now develop the ability to meet the threat of global terrorism wherever it may arise. This will no doubt be challenging, as the structure and strategy of the NATO alliance for decades has been to prepare for traditional conflict against the Soviet Union.

To meet the defense needs of today, all NATO nations will need to make a commitment to the forces and the resources that are necessary to root out and defeat state-sponsored and itinerant terrorism beyond the shores of the United States and Europe.

The seven nations that are poised to join NATO will be asked to take an immediate role in implementing this new mission. While it is unrealistic to ask these countries to meet the defense spending levels of the United States, the alliance should urge these new members to establish an expertise and an unmatched capability in a particular area of combating terrorism. NATO does not particularly need large, traditional forces or armaments. The alliance, rather, needs skilled units that can neutralize the devastating impacts of chemical or biological weapons, as well as seasoned intelligence organizations to ensure that NATO and its members are always able to thwart terrorist conspiracies or attacks before they are executed.

The seven aspirant countries have had to overcome significant political and economic difficulties to reach the precipice of NATO membership. Transforming a socialist-focused economy to one that is market based requires tremendous perseverance and visionary leadership and also an appreciation of liberty on the part of the people of these countries.

Indeed, the people of these nations have made their decisions and their choices. And now the economies of the aspirant countries are growing markets with potential for prosperous growth. These experiences will help these nations as they adjust to the burden of collective defense and make the responsible decisions that come with NATO membership.

I am confident that these countries—whether they are in the Baltics or Central Europe or Southeastern Europe—will continue to meet their responsibilities. You may ask, why are you so confident? Look at what these aspirant countries are already doing, and have been doing, in the current year and recent years. One must look only at the peacekeeping missions currently, and those that have been going on for several years in the Balkans.

You can look at the war in Afghanistan, and also the conflict in Iraq to conclude that not only will these nations be prepared to take the mantle of NATO membership—but are already contributing to the safety and security of all members. Their contributions and support have been substantive and significant in these current times of need.

NATO will certainly become a stronger alliance, with the capabilities and the vitality these prospective new members bring to the partnership.

I see these seven new members actually revitalizing NATO. There are concerns that have been expressed about the adherence and the unity of NATO. These seven countries will bring a revitalization, an appreciation for the importance of NATO and the freedoms and values we stand for.

When you discuss the expansion of NATO, the benefits of membership are often the focus. However, it is important to understand the tremendous value the alliance, and especially the United States, gains when these seven countries are offered membership.

We have seen the impact of these nations in the positions and actions taken during the recent military conflict in disarming Iraq. When the alliance first addressed the Iraq issue, it was these countries that immediately voiced their support for offering protection to an ally. Once the conflict began, these countries offered staging support as well as troops and chemical weapons teams which ensured Allied Forces were prepared to confront all possible battlefield scenarios. In particular, Bulgaria and Romania were helpful with their bases.

The alliance experienced a disconcerting event earlier this year when a member nation, Turkey, requested defense assistance. Critics again questioned the value and importance of NATO. However, those trying days highlighted the importance of this alliance to the United States. And while there was a small number of members who disagreed with the United States, the vast majority were in agreement with our policy and were extremely helpful in moving the alliance to assist Turkey in their defense needs.

Beyond the military conflict in Iraq, expanding the membership in NATO continues to be in the interest of this country. As the United States continues to confront terrorism on all fronts, we will need the continued support and intelligence assistance to make our efforts successful. Again, I feel confident these nations will take the lead in developing specialized programs that are needed within NATO.

Again, the aspirant countries are being asked to put together quick response forces to deal with chemical or biological attacks, should one occur. These are the invaluable programs that NATO will need as it changes its focus to fighting terrorism.

The United States will always need allies with which to partner to promote democratic values and our principles. By offering NATO membership to these seven countries, our country is gaining valuable allies that are intimately familiar with the value of individual freedom and also the concept of representative government. They appreciate what a blessing that is for the people.

The tremendous reforms and the progress that have been made by these aspirant nations is a testament to their commitment to the core values that have made NATO the strongest military alliance in history.

I strongly urge my colleagues to vote favorably on this resolution of ratification and welcome Bulgaria, Estonia, Latvia, Lithuania, Romania, Slovakia, and Slovenia to our alliance of shared security but, more importantly, to our alliance of shared values, principles, and aspirations for free people.

[Congressional Record: S5825-5826]

“ Taiwan, our ally and friend, is a democracy. …

The future of Taiwan must be determined

peacefully, with the express consent of the people

of Taiwan. Since its establishment, the United States

has been the foremost champion of liberty

and democracy in the world. ”

TAIWAN

February 5, 2004

Mr. President, for the past 54 years, Taiwan and the United States have been allies in the international arena, democratic partners and friends. In times of need and turmoil, both countries have always come to each other's aid. In the aftermath of the September 11 terrorist attacks, Taiwan immediately offered help to Americans through the U.S. Government. In recent months, Taiwan has offered humanitarian aid to post-war Iraq.

Today Taiwan is being threatened. Taiwan's planned referendum on March 20, 2004 has been called a move toward Taiwan independence. Some say it will push Taiwan to the "abyss of war." Such rhetoric is a distortion of Taiwan's true intentions. In the face of an overwhelming military threat against Taiwan, Taiwan President Chen Shui-bian's peace referendum asks Taiwan voters whether they should buy more anti-missile weapons if the People's Republic of China refuses to withdraw its 496 missiles targeted at Taiwan and whether Taiwan should open up talks with the People's Republic of China about issues of peace.

Taiwan's democratically elected president, President Chen, has made it clear that he continues to hold to the "five no's" of his inauguration speech, including the promise not to hold a plebiscite on the issue of Taiwanese independence. The referendum merely aims to avoid war, free its people from fear and maintain the status quo.

Taiwan, our ally and friend, is a democracy. Its people have every right to hold their referendum this March 20. Taiwan's referendum law is a basic democratic right that the United States should support rather than denigrate. The future of Taiwan must be determined peacefully, with the express consent of the people of Taiwan. Since its establishment, the United States has been the foremost champion of liberty and democracy in the world. We can, therefore, not afford to tell the people of Taiwan not to hold a referendum. There can be no double standard when it comes to exercising democracy.

[Congressional Record: S647]

" Cuba's human rights record remains poor. It continues to violate systematically the fundamental civil and political rights of its citizens. The State Department pointed out that the citizens of Cuba—as if we didn't know it already—do not have the right to change their government peacefully. The Government of Cuba does not allow criticism of the revolution four decades ago or its repressive, tyrannical leaders. "

CUBA

December 13, 2001

I have not had the opportunity in years past to hear the argument and debates on these issues. I consider these amendments to be very well founded. What they do is they have conditions for lifting restrictions on the financing of agricultural sales to Cuba, and two findings have to be made. The first condition is that the President must certify to Congress that convicted felons wanted by the FBI who are currently living as fugitives in Cuba have been returned to the United States for incarceration. I will not repeat all of the evidence in this regard that was previously cited by Senator Torricelli, Senator Nelson of Florida, and Senator Graham of Florida, concerning the return of criminals to the United States.

The second condition is that the President must certify to Congress that Cuba is not a state sponsor of international terrorism. That is the amendment of Senator Bob Smith.

Mr. President, I support fair and free trade and increased opportunities for U.S. workers and businesses, including our agricultural sector, to trade with other countries. However, prudence would lead us to seek to finance trade with countries that are not terrorist states. The Secretary of State maintains a list of countries that have repeatedly provided support for acts of international terrorism. Currently, there are seven countries on that State Department terrorism list. They are, in alphabetical order: Cuba, Iran, Iraq, Libya, North Korea, Sudan, and Syria. It is appropriate that Cuba is on that list.

Fidel Castro's regime has a long history of providing arms and training to terrorist organizations, many of which were articulated previously by Senator Graham. Our State Department notes that Havana remains a safe haven to several international terrorists and U.S. fugitives as well.

As we have seen since September 11, terrorists operate in an environment largely dominated by legally and geographically defined nation states. Terrorists sometimes rely on state-provided funding, bases, equipment, technical advice, logistical and support services.

In the wake of the September 11 terrorist attacks on the World Trade Center and Pentagon, President Bush, in addressing our Nation, stressed that the United States, in responding to these attacks, will make no distinction between the terrorists who committed these acts and those who harbor them. As we heard, the President characterized these terrorist acts as "acts of war."

An ongoing issue for our Congress and administration is how do we respond to state-sponsored or state-sanctioned terrorists and terrorism? There is no question that we need to respond. In my view, this country has dawdled along too many years not being worried about international terrorism, thinking that it would never affect us here at home. We have come to recognize that we must wage warfare against terrorists and those who aid, support, and comfort them.

An important part of that warfare is to oppose the terrorist states with every reasonable weapon at hand. That may be financial intercepts, surveillance, enhanced scrutiny of entrants into our country, infiltrating some of these terrorist organizations, greater intelligence here as well as abroad, military action when necessary, law enforcement abroad as well as here at home. All are components of our multifaceted war on terrorism.

Now, trade is also an important component of our current struggle against countries that are on the terrorism list.

Let's get into another aspect of Cuba. In February of this year, the State Department reported several salient facts about Cuba and life in Cuba for the people of Cuba, who we are purportedly trying to help. I do want to help the people of Cuba, but here is how we help them: First, let's recognize what they are facing.

Cuba's human rights record remains poor. It continues to violate systematically the fundamental civil and political rights of its citizens. The State Department pointed out that the citizens of Cuba—as if we didn't know it already—do not have the right to change their government peacefully.

The Government of Cuba does not allow criticism of the revolution four decades ago or its repressive, tyrannical leaders.

Cuba's laws against antigovernment statements and expressions of disrespect of Government officials carry penalties of between 3 months and 1 year in prison.

If Fidel Castro or members of the National Assembly or the Council of States are the objects of this criticism, the sentence for such expressions can be extended to 3 years in prison.

Recently, Fidel Castro was asked by Robert McNeill:

"Do you have political prisoners still in jail in Cuba?"

Castro responded:

"Yes, we have them. We have a few hundred political prisoners. Is that a violation of human rights?"

Well, I will answer Castro's rhetorical question. Yes, it is; darn right it is a violation of human rights. Castro's human rights practices are arbitrary and repressive. Hundreds of peaceful opponents of the Government remain imprisoned. Many thousands more are subject to short-term detentions, house arrest, surveillance, arbitrary searches, evictions, travel restrictions, politically motivated dismissals from employment, threats to them or their families, and other forms of harassment by the Cuban Government authorities.

Mr. President, let me repeat what our State Department said. Citizens of Cuba do not have the right to change their Government peacefully. Let us recall the words written 225 years ago by Thomas Jefferson in our Declaration of Independence:

"When a long train of abuses and usurpations ... evinces a design to reduce (people) under absolute Despotism, it is their right, it is their duty, to throw off such Government, and to provide new Guards for their future security."

Just as it was important for our ancestors to have the right to throw off the chains of the tyrannical monarchy 225 years ago, it must be the right of the Cuban people to free themselves of the chains of the tyrannical Castro regime.

Let us support the opportunities of the Cuban people to enjoy their unalienable rights to life, liberty, property, and the pursuit of happiness. Let us not retreat in our opposition to terrorism nor flinch from the advocacy of liberty.

[Congressional Record: S13107-13108]

May 14, 2002

Mr. President, many of us have anticipated the trip of former President Carter to Cuba with a mixed sense of hope and concern. We had hoped that he would use this unique opportunity to help bring ideas of freedom and democracy to the repressed people of Cuba, just 90 miles off our shores.

However, it was amazing and disappointing for many of us to learn of Mr. Carter's visit to a Cuban biotechnology facility and his acceptance, at face value, of the assurances of communist Cuban officials there that the facility is engaged solely in medical and humanitarian pursuits.

More distressing is that former President Jimmy Carter was accorded the same privilege and courtesy extended to former Presidents who have requested top-secret intelligence briefings and situation reports on global areas of interest of the United States.

In the post-9/11 world, it is important that we as a united country protect the safety and security of our people.

Instead, what we have in Mr. Carter's visit to this biotech facility is a former President—who himself was once responsible for our foreign policy and the safety of the American people—dismissing the concerns of his own government, revealing information to which he was privy in top-secret briefings, and buying wholesale the assertions of the dictator Fidel Castro and his minions.

The words and actions of Mr. Carter at this facility are a breach of trust, and it is made even worse, in that the individual involved in that breach is one in whom the American people once placed the ultimate trust and responsibility of the Presidency.

Rather than spending his time with Fidel Castro and his henceman, I would suggest the name of at least one person Mr. Carter would be better advised to get to know.

Just a few short days ago I joined the Congressional Cuba Political Prisoner Initiative. As part of this initiative, I have decided to sponsor or "adopt," if you will, a Cuban political prisoner named Francisco Chaviano Gonzales, and to advocate on his behalf, and on behalf of the thousands of others being held in Cuba in clear abuses of their basic human rights.

Francisco Chaviano is president of the National Council for Civil Rights, an organization dedicated to promoting democratic practices, racial equality and human rights. He was arrested after government agents broke into his home and confiscated documents revealing human rights abuses in Cuba—specifically, information about the Castro government's sinking of a tugboat that claimed the lives of 41 men, women, and children who were attempting to escape to freedom.

Chaviano was arrested and detained in prison for 1 year, and although a civilian, he was tried by military tribunal and sentenced to 15 years in prison.

He has been confined in isolation and deprived of basic medical care for long periods of time. After being allowed to visit him for the first time in eight years, his wife reported that he is in very poor health. Other members of the civil rights organization have followed in Chaviano's footsteps and continued to press the Cuban government for democratic reforms, at great peril to themselves.

Jimmy Carter is a man who is often praised in the media as a "model ex-President" or a "statesman" for his work with Habitat for Humanity. I do believe there is still time for him to make a more positive contribution to the plight of the Cuban people and to American foreign policy regarding Fidel Castro.

Mr. Carter is scheduled to deliver a speech to the Cuban people tonight. His remarks have the potential to do enormous good or to cause further harm. Rather than legitimizing a tyrant and a man who doesn't care for the well-being of his own people; he could advocate positive change for the beleaguered Cuban people.

If Mr. Carter in his speech tonight is looking for a road map to freedom and prosperity for the Cuban people, he need look no further than the words and principles of freedom written by George Mason in the Virginia Declaration of Rights. This document, adopted on June 12, 1776, helped form the basis of our Declaration of Independence and 15 years later in our Bill of Rights as the first amendments to our Constitution.

I would read a few excerpts from George Mason's historic words from various articles of the Virginia Declaration of Rights, which I think are instructive.

"Article 1: That all men are by nature equally free and independent and have certain inherent rights, of which, when they enter into a state of society, they cannot, by any compact, deprive or divest their posterity; namely, the enjoyment of life and liberty, with the means of acquiring and possessing property, and pursuing and obtaining happiness and safety.

"Article 2: That all power is vested in, and consequently derived from, the people; that magistrates are their trustees and servants and at all times amenable to them.

"Article 3: That government is, our ought to be, instituted for the common benefit, protection, and security of the people, nation, or community; of all the various modes and forms of government, that is best which is capable of producing the greatest degree of happiness and safety and is most effectually secured against the danger of maladministration. And that, when any government shall be found inadequate or contrary to these purposes, a majority of the community has an indubitable, inalienable, and indefeasible right to reform, alter, or abolish it, in such manner as shall be judged most conductive to the public weal.

"Article 12: That the freedom of the press is one of the great bulwalks of liberty, and can never be restrained but by despotic governments.

"Article 16: That religion, or the duty which we owe to our Creator, and the manner of discharging it, can be directed only by reason and conviction, not by force or violence; and therefore all men are equally entitled to the free exercise of religion, according to the dictates of conscience ..."

Those are the words of freedom, and of the inherent rights to which all people are entitled, even if only temporarily subjugated.

Therefore, I call on former President Carter to embrace these truths and to use this unique opportunity to advance these enduring principles of liberty in Cuba.

I urge him to support the Varela Project, which is a petition drive that has collected the 10,000 signatures needed under Castro's so-called "constitution" to force a referendum on whether his government should be allowed to continue.

I call on Fidel Castro to heed the concepts first enunciated by George Mason 226 years ago in the Western Hemisphere, and I also call upon him to schedule free and fair democratic elections on the island of Cuba within the next year.

Mr. President, I will close with more words from George Mason, who said:

"There is a passion to the mind of man, especially a free man, which renders him impatient of a restraint."

Mr. Carter has the power to either to fan the flames of those passions and aspirations of the Cuban people, or to throw cold water on them. The choice he needs to make is clear. Do not flinch. Stand strong for freedom!

[Congressional Record: S4326-4327]

April 6, 2005

Madam President, I rise to urge my colleagues to oppose this amendment and continue to support our country's investment in television broadcasting into Cuba. Otherwise known as TV Martí. The Senator from North Dakota may be exaggerating, and folks get carried away as well. He will say that this is not needed. This is needed. There may be a question as to how effective the TV Martí signal is getting in to Cuba.

Because we are talking about signals and broadcasts, let's make sure we are sending the right signal here. Whether it is my good friend from Oregon or whether my friend from North Dakota, we all, I would hope, want to make sure we are standing strong on the ability of people who are repressed and under the tyranny of Castro, to get information.

There are questions as to whether all the ways that we are trying to get around the jamming and scrambling of signals by Castro's regime are effective or not; however, it is a matter of our national interest that we try to get information, objective information, to the people of Cuba. It doesn't matter one's culture. All human beings, no matter their background or culture, if given the choice, the opportunity, will choose freedom. We have seen it with the Afghan people. We have seen it with the people in Iraq. We are seeing it with the Lebanese rising up to get the Syrian troops out. We have seen it with the Palestinians, with the death of the corrupt terrorist Arafat. The same applies to the people of Cuba, or anywhere else in the world. The Cuban people share the desire that all human beings have, and that is a need to have information and an opportunity to determine their own destiny.

I believe that Radio Martí and TV Martí can help promote freedom and justice in Cuba. We all know the United States has sponsored television and radio broadcasting in Cuba for almost 20 years. The effect of all of that— and we can all try to find measurements. It is not as if you can go around Cuba and do surveys. This is not allowed. Remember, this is Castro's regime. If I want some evidence of a probative witness, I am going to listen to the Senator from Florida, Mr. Martinez, who made history, standing here as the first person ever born in Cuba to be elected to serve in the U.S. Senate. He understands the impact of our message to Cuba better than anybody or any statistics one would want to put forth.

So while we understand it is very difficult to get into Cuba and make sure of the effectiveness of TV or radio broadcasts, it is well known that Radio Martí—and to the extent we can get TV Martí in—is looked upon as an authoritative and reliable source of accurate, objective, and comprehensive news for the Cuban people.

If this Congress were to eliminate TV Martí, we would be sending the wrong message to the Cuban people. At a time when freedom is on the march around the world, eliminating TV Martí would tell the Cuban people—I suspect Castro would be getting his minions and fellow thugs of that regime out to say the United States isn't going to bother. We succeeded with jamming or scrambling the signals, saying the United States doesn't want to worry about this. It would be a signal for him to say that the United States is not committed to the cause of freedom in Cuba. Of course, with his long history of repressing free speech and the free flow of information and ideas in Cuba, this plays right into Castro's hands.

Thomas Jefferson once said:

"A free people [claim] their rights as derived from the laws of nature, and not as a gift of their chief magistrate."

The sharing of information and free flow of ideas, and the foundation of any free country is not to be something that is given or taken away by the machinations of a dictator like Castro.

In my view, there are four pillars of a free and just society. This is how I measure freedom myself for people if they are living in a free and just society. The first pillar is freedom of religion, where people's rights are not enhanced or diminished because of religious beliefs; second, freedom of expression; third, private ownership of property; fourth, the rule of law, where disputes are adjudicated fairly and God-given rights are protected. The second pillar, freedom of expression, is absolutely essential, where people are allowed to get information and to think for themselves. To communicate not in a way that is harmful, but the God-given rights of expression being protected.

We have to support the opportunity of the people of Cuba to get information. They are not going to get it from their Government. People will say, gosh, we are having to use airplanes. There are different ways you have to get at it. You cannot use balloons or a dirigible; you cannot do it off of broadcasting. Why can't we use it the way everybody else sees TV? It is because of that regime. Sometimes you have to be more clever than some of the reptilian cutthroats that we are dealing with. In my view, we ought to stand for the concept of freedom of expression. We have seen it work and we have seen it on Radio Martí. I hate wasting money, but there are certain things we need to do. This is actually a less expensive way of advocating freedom, by using technology—using extraordinary means, but still getting the message to the people of Cuba, regardless of the obstacles that are established by Castro's regime. I think we need to be providing news, commentary, and promoting the open exchange of information and ideas in Cuba and elsewhere to promote the cause of freedom.

To be effective in further opening communications and the sharing of ideas throughout Cuba, Radio and TV Martí must continue to be broadcast and should receive our country's support. I sincerely urge my colleagues to oppose this amendment and stand with the Senator from Florida, Mr. Martinez, but, most importantly, stand for the advancement of freedom.

[Congressional Record: S3246]

"We need a new approach toward Damascus. Continuation of the current U.S. policy toward Syria must end. For too long, it has been too ineffective and has allowed Syria to pursue with near impunity policies counter to U.S. interests. Moreover, it is unproductive and antithetical to the principles associated with the President's war on terrorism."

S Y R I A

November 11, 2003

M r. President, for decades, the United States has engaged the regime in Syria in the hope that Damascus would play a constructive role in bringing about Arab-Israeli peace. The U.S.-Syria relationship has been ongoing despite the fact that Syria has been ruled by dictatorship with an uninterrupted record of support for terrorism, specifically directed at Israel.

The results of U.S. engagement with Syria have been anything but positive. Throughout the years, Damascus has continued to support international terrorism directed at America and Israel, occupy Lebanon, develop a weapons-of-mass-destruction program, acquire ballistic missiles, and pursue policies counter to U.S. interests.

Since the liberation of Iraq, Syria has played a destabilizing role by allowing terrorist fugitives to enter Syria and by allowing mercenaries to cross into Iraq—or at least not stopping them—to engage U.S. troops. Syria has been able to conduct its policies—which are antithetical to U.S. interests—with near impunity. They have resulted in the loss of hundreds of American lives—especially when you consider the bombing of the U.S. Marine Corps barracks in Beirut in 1983.

Although Syria is listed—and has been since the 1970s—by the State Department as a state sponsor of terrorism, along with Iran, Libya, Iraq, Cuba, and North Korea, it has not faced the same degree of diplomatic and economic isolation that has been directed at other terrorist states. In fact, Washington maintains full diplomatic relations with Syria, making Syria the only designated state sponsor of terrorism to have such relations with the United States.

Syria's special treatment despite its support for terrorism should be over.

The events of September 11, 2001 have offered a window of opportunity to review many U.S. bilateral relationships and determine whether it is necessary to change the dynamic—and often the status quo—that has characterized these relations. The administration and Congress have done this most notably with Saudi Arabia in seeking greater cooperation in the elimination of terrorist activities operating from Saudi soil.

Now is also an ideal time to reassess U.S. relations with Damascus and demand accountability in our relationship. Equally important, it is time for the Syrian leadership to make a tough choice: it is either with the United States completely in the war on terrorism, or it is not. Either way, shielding Syria from the same economic and political isolation directed at other terrorist states is unmerited and runs counter to U.S. principles in the war against terrorism.

As Under Secretary of State John Bolton stated in testimony before the House International Relations Committee on September 16, 2003, "Syria remains a security concern on two important counts: terrorism and weapons of mass destruction." Bolton added: There is no graver threat to our country today than states that both sponsor terrorism and possess or aspire to possess weapons of mass destruction. Syria, which offers physical sanctuary and political protection to groups such as Hezbollah, Hamas, and Palestinian Jihad, and whose terrorist operations have killed hundreds of innocent people— including Americans—falls into this category of state of potential dual threat.

Since the 1970s, the U.S. State Department has listed Syria as a state sponsor of terrorism. Specifically, in its "Patterns of Global Terrorism, 2002" report, the State Department found that the Syrian Government "has continued to provide political and limited material support to a number of Palestinian groups, including allowing them to maintain headquarters or offices in Damascus," although the Syrian Government insists that the groups' Damascus offices undertake only political and informational activities, not terrorist operations.

Syria maintains close relations with Iran, another autocratic regime listed by the State Department as a state sponsor of terrorism and a prominent financial, political, and military backer of these Palestinian terrorist organizations.

Moreover, Syria remains the de facto ruler of Lebanon, which it has forcibly and illegally occupied since 1990. Lebanon, the country in which more than 200 U.S. Marines died in 1983 following a terrorist attack on their Beirut barracks, remains a breeding ground and training center for terrorist organizations.

Terrorism has spawned in Syria due largely to Syria's opposition to the existence of Israel and its subsequent objection to an Arab-Israeli peace process. Although the United States has engaged Syria—and given it a prominent place in discussions—during the past few decades, Damascus has long been an unwilling and uncooperative partner in bringing about Middle East peace. In fact, Syria did not endorse President Bush's Middle East "roadmap."

Syria also appears to be in the terror financing business. In April 2003, an Italian government study found that Syria functioned as a hub for an al-Qaida network that moved Islamic extremists and funds from Italy to northeastern Iraq, where the recruits fought alongside the recently defeated Ansar al Islam terrorist group.

And, on October 21, it was reported that U.S. Treasury Department investigators have evidence that $3 billion that belonged to Saddam Hussein's government is being held in Syria-controlled banks in Syria and Lebanon. The Syrian Government has not yet granted Treasury officials access to these accounts, nor has it been willing to share any information about the account holders.

Let's review past U.S. policy toward Damascus. Despite all of Syria's irresponsible and threatening policies, successive U.S. administrations have been willing to engage the Syrian Government. For decades, the United States has pursued a policy of engagement with Syria, trying to win Damascus' support for Middle East peace but to no avail.

As part of this strategy, the United States has maintained full diplomatic relations with Damascus. It also has allowed U.S. companies to invest in Syria, something that cannot be done in other terrorist-sponsor states such as North Korea, Iran, Cuba, and Libya.

According to the Congressional Research Service, in 1999—the last year there was reliable data available—direct investment of U.S. companies into Syria was $6 million, with 13 U.S. businesses having offices in Syria. While this may seem miniscule in terms of the dollar amount, it is notable because it is tolerated at all.

With the death of Syrian President Hafez Assad in 2000 and the ascendancy of his son Bashar to the presidency, there were high expectations that Syria would depart from its anti-Israeli policies and pro-terrorist support of the past and enact political and economic reforms, as well as become a positive influence and player in achieving Middle East peace. Three years into Bashar's term, such developments have not materialized—and without a catalyst to encourage such reform, it appears unlikely that Bashar will proactively change Syria's course.

We need a new approach toward Damascus. Continuation of the current U.S. policy toward Syria must end. For too long, it has been too ineffective and has allowed Syria to pursue with near impunity policies counter to U.S. interests. Moreover, it is unproductive and antithetical to the principles associated with the President's war on terrorism.

The U.S. must pressure Syria to play by the rules. Given that the government of Syrian President Bashar al-Assad is relatively weak, and recognizing that Bashar deemed it necessary, or least desirable, to provide some assistance to the United States in apprehending al-Qaida, it should be possible to pressure Damascus into changing its policies. That said, Washington must demonstrate that it is serious about having Damascus drop its support of terrorism and its pursuit of policies that endanger peace and stability in the Middle East.

Therefore, to demonstrate American commitment, the United States should adopt the following measures in pressuring Syria: Enact the Syria Accountability Act now. Among the numerous provisions contained in the bill, the most notable include the calls for Syria to immediately and unconditionally halt support for terrorism; withdraw from Lebanon and provide for Lebanon's full restoration of sovereignty; halt development of certain weapons; and enter into serious unconditional bilateral peace negotiations with Israel.

This bill also states that Syria "should bear responsibility for attacks committed by Hezbollah and other terrorist groups with offices, training camps, or other facilities" in Syria or Lebanon. Further, the bill states, that being in violation of key United Nations Security Council resolutions and pursuing policies which undermine international peace and security, "Syria should not have been permitted to join the United Nations Security Council or serve as the Security Council's President, and should be removed from the Security Council."

Pursuant to the legislation, the United States is empowered to "will work to deny Syria the ability to support acts of terrorism and efforts to acquire weapons of mass destruction, WMD." In addition, the United States will not provide any assistance to Syria and will oppose all forms of multilateral assistance to Syria until Damascus withdraws from Lebanon and halts its pursuit of WMD and ballistic missile accumulation.

Until Syria enacts these measures, the President is required to prohibit: the sale of defense articles to Syria that require the issuance of an export license—dual-use items; U.S. businesses from investing in Syria; and export of any goods other than food and medicine to Syria. Diplomatic relations also must be reduced but the degree of that is not defined. The President is given waiver authority for 6-month periods for all of these categories, except the export of dual-use items if it is determined that "it is in the vital national security interest" to do so.

The Bush administration should apply uniformity in its policies toward terrorist-sponsoring states. Therefore, the administration should not allow U.S. companies to invest in Syria because it sends the signal that Syria is receiving special treatment from Washington. A fairly dramatic reduction of U.S. diplomatic representation would perhaps strongly suggest to Syria that it is not an American ally and will not be one until it starts acting like one.

Sending a strong message is key.

The United States should apply the proliferation security initiative, PSI, and sanction WMD suppliers. The administration has successfully developed and employed a plan, known as the proliferation security initiative, PSI, to interdict illicit weapons shipments and contraband. PSI was announced by President Bush on May 31, 2003. It involves robust cargo inspections and possible interdiction of WMD materials and illegal arms, based on pooled intelligence among participating countries. To date, 11 nations form the core PSI group: Britain, France, Germany, Australia, Japan, Italy, Spain, Portugal, Poland, the Netherlands, and the United States. While most of the initial PSI activities have focused on North Korea, attention should be paid to Syria—and Iran—with the goal of halting the flow of weapons technology both in and out of Syria.

A critical complementary strategy to PSI is using sanctions on countries that supply Syria with weapons and WMD technology. The People's Republic of China, Pakistan, Russia, Iran, and North Korea are known proliferators of these materials, with Russia and North Korea being key suppliers to Syria.

As part of a wider U.S. policy, the administration should attempt to convince its PSI allies to also use sanctions against WMD suppliers.

In conclusion, Syria's actions in the Middle East—and in Iraq, specifically pose a clear, near-term threat to regional stability and to the safety and security of American forces serving in the region.

With the removal of Saddam Hussein's regime in Iraq and the defeat of the Taliban regime in Afghanistan, the United States has made clear that state support for terrorism will no longer be tolerated.

It is overdue for the United States and like-minded nations to hold Syria accountable for its actions. Syria's new head of state has had ample time to make the choice whether Damascus is with the United States as a partner or not in fighting the war on terrorism.

If Syria is not, then it should face the diplomatic and economic consequences as set out in the Syria Accountability Act. As a sponsor of the Senate version, S. 982, I respectfully urge my colleagues to vote for this important measure in the form of H.R. 1828, as amended.

[Congressional Record: S14413-14414]

"Never forget. We will never forget. We will always remember this day that forged America together. These horrific events have strengthened our unity of purpose and resolve as Americans, that we stand strong together for liberty. I hope and pray that as long as God continues to bless our United States and indeed blesses the entire world with people of such courage, integrity, and character, that liberty and justice will endure and prevail."

ATTACKS OF
SEPTEMBER 11, 2001

September 12, 2001

M r. President, my fellow Members of the Senate, this is a very sad day as we witness all of the implications and tragedies and lives lost from yesterday's dastardly terrorist attacks on the United States.

Yesterday's attacks were attacks not just on the United States and our particular Commonwealth of Virginia or State of New York; it is an attack on freedom-loving people and everything we stand for as a unique and great nation.

On Monday afternoon, Senator Boxer and I were ready to introduce a resolution condemning the suicide bombings in the Middle East.

We would have introduced that resolution on Monday, but wanted to include another clause recognizing the attacks in Israel on Sunday. We now see with great shock and horror, that the United States is obviously not impervious to these suicide bombings and such attacks.

What we need to do now is coalesce, coalesce as a people with our shared beliefs, coalesce to comfort those who have lost loved ones and then also determine where we need to go to move forward to try to prevent such acts from occurring in the future. Our goal and focus right now must be on the rescue, hoping there are those who are still alive. Secondly, we need to find as many details and information as to how our security was breached so as to hopefully prevent it in the future. And thirdly of course, hold those who are responsible accountable and bring them to justice.

We are hearing stories just in the first day of great heroes. Heroes in New York. People who knew that the building was going to collapse, but nevertheless stayed there trying to usher people out. On C-SPAN this morning, one of those who was just a volunteer helper knew what was going on, where those who were emergency and federal FBI agents were as well, knowing that the building was going to collapse, staying there knowing those were the last minutes of their life trying to save people.

The same was happening in Virginia where we have lost many lives, untold numbers, as of yet, at the Pentagon as well as the passengers on flight 77 flying from Dulles, VA, that was hijacked and crashed into the Pentagon.

There are great stories of bravery, with people going above and beyond what is expected, and that should give us comfort as a nation. This tragedy has affected many lives, and we still don't know how many lives. It will probably take a week if not weeks to determine how many lives have been lost. Even in the small neighborhood where we live, where my daughter goes to middle school, children were crying because their parents work at the Pentagon. Others work at Fort Belvoir and there was worry that Fort Belvoir was being hit. There's only maybe a couple of dozen houses in our development, but a youngster—who came by our house to get to know my children, his father was on Flight 77.

So, as the days go forward, we are all going to be learning these stories of innocent people whose lives have been lost and the families that will forever be scarred with the loss of that loved one. Our thoughts and prayers must be with those families. Whether they're in New York or people who are from Connecticut or New Jersey, people from Virginia, here in the D.C. area, I'm sure there are folks from Maryland and the District, clearly people from Massachusetts were on the hijacked flight from Boston. Clearly a lot of people from California, since the destination of all of those flights was to be California.

This is truly a day that will live in infamy. History will record these as the most violent, insane, cowardly acts that have ever been perpetrated on our homeland in the United States of America. We need to be united, coalesced as Americans, but also with our allies in our resolve, our resolve to pursue these cowardly conspirators who perpetrated these murderous acts.

In our response to justice, we need to be sure, we need to be swift, and we need to be severe. In my view, we have allowed terrorism to go on too long, thinking that we could be immune from it. But nevertheless, we need to recognize that we're going to have to wage warfare.

These people have struck against the symbol of American strength and power. They are not, though, going to be able to weaken the will of the people of the United States. We will stay united, defending our interests and our principles. We will also stick together, not just as Virginians and New Yorkers, but as Americans aiding and helping the families who have lost loved ones in whatever they can do.

The senior Senator from Virginia, John Warner, and I will work together to make sure that for those Federal employees that the Government is doing all they can as well as for the civilian employees. And it is not just as Virginians. I know that the Presiding Officer, sitting there from Florida, cares just as much as anybody else does.

And so we are all going to stick together in that regard. We do need to learn from this, though. And as we learn, we must make sure that as we learn the facts, we do not allow these attacks to succeed in tempting us in any way to diminish what makes us a great nation. And what makes us a great nation is that this is a country that understands that people have God-given rights and liberties. And we cannot—in our efforts to bring justice—diminish those liberties.

Clearly, this is not a simple, normal criminal case. This is an act of war, and those rules apply. But at home and domestically, we need to make sure that we are not tempted to abrogate any civil rights such as habeas corpus or protections against unreasonable searches and seizures, or the freedom of expression and peaceable assembly, freedom of religion. And just because somebody may come from an ethnic background, that means nothing. They are American citizens. And so let's make sure that in our anger and in our efforts to bring justice, we remember our basic foundational civil liberties and do not abrogate them.

We are a nation of laws, of good-hearted people, of loving people. And so I would say in closing, Mr. President, let's make sure we pray for and comfort those who have lost loved ones.

Let's get the facts, move swiftly and properly. But most importantly, as Americans, let's stay strong. Let's stay resolved, and let's keep moving forward. Because, indeed, all the world is watching, not just the Senate; they are watching the United States and Americans. What will their response be? Let's keep moving forward. We are the beacon for freedom-loving people in the world, sticking together we will persevere. We will bring justice. And we will come out safer and stronger in the end.

[Congressional Record: S9289]

September 11, 2002

Mr. President, I rise today to offer my thoughts on this very solemn day of remembrance as we all return from a magnificent ceremony at the Pentagon observing all that is strong and good and awesome about our country.

I thank the Senator from Nevada for his very poignant words of empathy, as well as his understanding of the foundations of our country. Nevada, as all States, was hit hard.

We saw the outpouring of compassion all over this country, and I will share some of those stories. I recall in August driving across a lonely two-lane road in South Dakota, which would eventually get to the Badlands. There was a big bale of hay on the side of the road which had painted on it the American flag. It showed the spirit of that farm. We did not see any people, but we knew the sentiment of the folks who lived on that farm and in that region.

September 11, 9/11, just those words evoke sentiments and memories of where we were and what we did on that day of tragedy. As we remember those vile terrorist attacks of one year ago, for many of us the emotions and shock, the disbelief and horror that we experienced individually and as a people and a nation are still fresh. Those memories, however, continue to strengthen our resolve in the same way that our Nation was forged together after those vile attacks a year ago.

Today, we view our Nation in a fundamentally new light. We have a greater understanding of the freedoms we enjoy and how vital it is that they be guarded, preserved, and even fought for, if necessary. We have a greater appreciation for a country that respects people of diverse backgrounds, cultures, and religious beliefs. We have poured out our hearts and our assistance to those who were injured and the families of those who lost a dear one. We view firefighters, police officers, first responders, with much greater appreciation, whether they are the brave men and women of the battalions in New York City or northern Virginia or in communities large and small all across our United States of America. These men and women were transformed on that day into our heroes. We will forever remember the thousands of innocent men, women, and children who were killed at the World Trade Center and in a field in Somerset County, PA.

This Senator will remember the 184 patriots at the Pentagon and on American Airlines flight 77 who lost their lives on Virginia soil. It is indeed the heroes and the innocent patriotic victims we will remember the most. The images of flags raised, the solemn salute of rescuers to their fallen comrades, and people who were rushing into burning buildings on the verge of collapsing hoping to just save one more life.

They and the freedom-loving patriots across our great Nation stand in stark contrast to those who only know hate, destruction, and oppression.

We also see that in a time of trial, ordinary people of all walks of life perform with extraordinary courage and dignity. We remember people such as LTC Ted Anderson, who carried two of the injured from the burning Pentagon and reentered through a broken window to drag out two more, one whose clothes were on fire; 1SG Rick Keevill and Virginia State Troopers Mike Middleton and Myrlin Wimbish, who entered the Pentagon three separate times looking for victims; LCDR David Tarantino, who moved a pile of rubble enough to pull a man from the Pentagon just before the roof collapsed; other Pentagon heroes such as SSG Christopher Braman; LTC Victor Correa; SGT Roxane Cruz-Cortes; MAJ John Grote; LTC Robert Grunewald; COL Philip McNair; CPT Darrell Oliver; SP Michael Petrovich; SGM Tony Rose; LTC Marilyn Wills; and CPT David Thomas.

The Senator from Nevada, Mr. Reid, mentioned a woman who I think was Mrs. Kurtz at the Pentagon. Mrs. Louise Kurtz, though severely burned herself, valiantly tended to the needs of others around her. I am introducing legislation that will change current law so that individuals—such as Mrs. Kurtz, and those in her situation—can contribute to her retirement and so they will be able to afford to return to work after a very lengthy period of recuperation.

We also remember people such as Barbara Olson, a passenger on flight 77 who had the presence of mind to call loved ones on the ground to alert them of the hijacking.

We remember CPT "Chic" Burlingame of flight 77 who died fighting off hijackers who commandeered his plane and who is now properly buried at Arlington National Cemetery. These people have all touched our lives.

In talking to Mr. Burlingame's brothers and sister and wife, I find it noteworthy that at the Arlington National Cemetery his grave is on the tour and people in the tradition of those of the Jewish faith will put rocks on his headstone. That is very touching to the family and shows the unity and appreciation of a grateful nation.

We also remember the survivors, survivors such as Stephen Push, whose wife Lisa Raines perished in the Pentagon and who has become a forceful and articulate spokesman for victims and families.

I will always remember, and thought of it last night while driving home, a young boy, a neighbor, a friend of my children whose name is Nick Jacoby. He lost his father on flight 77.

There are stories all over our communities and Nation. We also, of course, remember the quiet dignity of people such as Lisa Beamer who helped keep their loved ones very much alive for all of us. Her husband Todd, who said, "Let's roll," led an uprising with several other patriots against the hijackers of flight 93 and saved hundreds, if not thousands, of lives at the Capitol and in the Washington, DC, area.

Recent reports recognize their likely target was this building.

We will remember countless others whose courageous efforts saved lives and provided comfort. We will remember and we will thank them for their extraordinary, inspirational dignity and their character. We will also remember the construction workers, the hard-hat patriots of the Phoenix project who worked around the clock in their inspiring efforts to rebuild the Pentagon in plenty of time for employees to move in before the 1-year anniversary.

We will remember folks from a church that made quilts, the Christ Baptist Church from Prince William in Manassas, a magnificent quilt with the names of all who died. Also, we will remember the International House of Pancakes in Bristol, VA, an IHOP owned by an American who came here from Lebanon. I asked him a few months later how his business was. He said right after the attacks, for a few weeks, there were hardly any customers. But then a Methodist Church in Bristol, on the Virginia-Tennessee line, brought up the situation, and everyone from that church on that Sunday went in with their families and filled up the IHOP. Since then, others were coming back. That is a sign of the decency and the care of communities across the Nation.

Five days ago, in New York City, I had the opportunity to speak to a group of 70 mothers who were pregnant last September 11, and who were made widows on that terrible day. It has been said that suffering makes kinsmen of us all. While those mothers no longer have the physical and emotional support of their husbands, and the fathers of their children, they are now a part of our greater American family. In those babies, all under 1 year, the spirit and blood of their fathers live on. We want the babies to grow up with the optimism of liberty and opportunity and hope that is the spirit of America. These young children represent not just a birth but a rebirth, a rebirth and a rededication of the strength and unity of our Nation and her great, caring people as we move forward. Indeed, our Nation will be changed for generations by the tragic events of a single day and all those that followed September 11. We pray for the souls of all that we lost that day and their surviving families as well. ...

Never forget. We will never forget. We will always remember this day that forged America together. These horrific events have strengthened our unity of purpose and resolve as Americans, that we stand strong together for liberty. I hope and pray that as long as God continues to bless our United States and indeed blesses the entire world with people of such courage, integrity, and character, that liberty and justice will endure and prevail.

[Congressional Record: S8476-8477]

September 11, 2003

Mr. President, it is altogether fitting that we have finally accomplished this idea on the second anniversary of the violent and dastardly attacks of September 11, 2001. Several survivors of that tragic day helped inspire this legislation, which will adjust Federal employees' retirement computations to offset reductions in the retirement amounts arising from on-the-job injuries covered under the workers compensation program. ...

Mr. President, this bill addresses a problem in the retirement program for Federal employees that has been recognized for a long time but unresolved since 1986, when the current retirement system was established. Unfortunately, complications arising from the Tax Code and the Workers Rehabilitation Act of 1973 have blocked any solution.

My resolve to introduce this bill and address this problem was inspired by Ms. Louise Kurtz, a Federal employee from Virginia who was severely injured in the September 11 attack, 2 years ago today, on the Pentagon. She worked at the Pentagon as a civil service employee. She suffered burns from the impact of American Airlines Flight 77, but even with all these burns, she still was trying to rescue and help others get out. She suffered burns on over 70 percent of her body. I have seen her several times. In fact, I saw her last year, at the Project Phoenix, the reopening and dedication of the Pentagon. She had no fingers left—just little nubs, really. Her ears were mostly burned off as well. She is a person, though, who continues to endure these painful surgeries and faces other surgeries in the future. She wants to continue with her rehabilitation. She still hopes to return to work someday.

Current law, however, does not allow Mrs. Kurtz to contribute to her retirement program while she is recuperating and receiving workers compensation disability payments. As a result, after returning to work and eventually retiring, she will find herself inadequately prepared and unable to afford to retire because of the lack of contributions during her recuperation and rehabilitation.

As Mrs. Kurtz's situation reveals, Federal employees under the Federal employees retirement system who have sustained an on-the-job injury and are receiving disability compensation from the Department of Labor's Office of Workers Compensation Programs are unable to make contributions or payments into Social Security or the Thrift Savings Plan. Therefore, under the current situation, which is being changed by this law, future retirement benefits from both sources—the Thrift Savings Plan and Social Security—are reduced.

This legislation offsets the reductions in Social Security and the Thrift Savings Plan retirement benefits by increasing the Federal Employees Retirement System's direct benefit calculation by 1 percentage point for the extended periods of disability.

Mr. President, you have probably already heard my talk about this bill because we have actually passed this measure twice in the Senate. We passed it once on October 17, 2002, and then again in July of this year, 2003. As a lead sponsor of the bill, I was pleased to see that my colleague on the House side, Congresswoman Jo Ann Davis, with her persistence, finally got the House of Representatives to pass this measure yesterday. By taking this matter up and passing it in the Senate today, we are clearing it for the President's signature.

The passage of this bill ensures that the pensions of our hard-working Federal employees will be kept whole during a period of injury and recuperation, especially now that many of them are on the front lines in protecting our homeland security in this new and ongoing war against terror. By protecting the retirement security of injured Federal employees, we have provided an incentive for them to return to work and increased our ability to retain our most dedicated and experienced Federal workers. This is a reasonable and fair approach, in which the whole Senate acted in a logical and compassionate manner last fall, and, of course, we did so in July, and we have done so again today.

On the second anniversary of the attacks on the World Trade Center, the Pentagon, and Flight 93, which crashed in Pennsylvania after the brave efforts of those passengers, I thank my colleagues for once again passing this compassionate legislation honoring and helping some of the survivors of these horrific events.

[Congressional Record: S11424]

September 10, 2004

M<small>r.</small> President, I rise this afternoon to offer my thoughts on the eve of the third anniversary of the September 11, 2001, terrorist attacks. Rather than show divisiveness and criticism, or talk about politics, I think it is important to reflect on how much that tragedy has changed our lives and challenged all of us—not just Republicans, not just Democrats, but all Americans—to do all that we can to protect all that is good and wholesome about America.

Tomorrow, Saturday, American families will be doing what they have done for generations in the early fall. In Charlottesville, the University of Virginia will be hosting the Tar Heels from North Carolina; in Columbia, SC, the University of Georgia football team will be playing the Gamecocks of South Carolina; in Richmond, Saturday night, there will be more than 100,000 fans there for the big NASCAR race; at the wonderful and traditional Wrigley Field in Chicago, the Cubs will be playing the Florida Marlins; and families, in the afternoon, will be having cookouts in their backyards; others will be gathered as a family at their dinner tables.

During all of these wonderful, truly American events, we will all pause to remember a day when such innocence was shattered by the vile, hate-filled attacks on our homeland that manifested themselves so viciously in New York City, at the Pentagon in Arlington, VA, and in Somerset County, PA. We will remember the loss of 3,000 Americans that day, and we will pray for their souls and certainly pray for their families. We will remember friends and we will remember neighbors lost on that day.

At all of those sporting events, when the National Anthem is sung, I venture to guess that song will be sung with greater vigor, more loudly, and with greater patriotism than one would normally hear. When they conclude those final lines talking about how we are the "land of the free," and because we are the "home of the brave," we will be thinking of our troops who are serving and protecting us in precarious positions in Afghanistan, Iraq, and prosecuting the war on terrorism.

In some ways, September 11, 2001, seems a long time ago. Yet we have done so much in only a few years, and we will continue to do so in the future, to prevent such attacks on America.

Our focus in Government and our private lives has obviously profoundly changed. We see it with our fortified airports, greater protection in our public buildings, our shipping ports, and even cyberspace.

We have strengthened and updated law enforcement capabilities and intelligence, and our work on the Senate floor in the next few weeks will further enhance those efforts with meaningful improvements and the use of innovations of technology to better gather and analyze counterterrorism information.

We have been more vigilant in watching enemies and threats at home and abroad. We have intercepted financial assistance to terrorists.

Yes, through it all, the fabric of our Nation has become stronger and more appreciated as we face these unprecedented challenges. Our resolve and our focus is more clear. Our determination to protect freedoms here and around the world is greater than ever before.

We are so appreciative of the men and women in uniform who are protecting us, whether in Afghanistan or Iraq or on ships around the world. For our security, they are taking the offensive to the terrorists overseas. We are grateful for those who are active or maybe in the Guard or in the Reserves, or their employers here at home. Of course, we are so grateful to their families who have sent their sons and daughters, their loved ones and their friends overseas to protect us.

Our economic ingenuity, our competitiveness, our strength is being rekindled and reignited by free people and free enterprise. In many ways, those who brought us harm on September 11 surely miscalculated the character of the American people. We are a Nation of bravery and heroism.

I will never forget the stories about the first responders in New York City going into the Trade Centers, breathing their last breaths of life trying to save a few more innocent victims. The same with the Pentagon. The responders came in not only from Arlington but all over northern Virginia, from Maryland, and even some from the District of Columbia, rushing into acrid, toxic air, trying to save those who had been hit, whether on the plane, but mostly those who were the surviving or people working at the Pentagon. These people ignored their personal safety. They rushed into harm's way to help their fellow Americans on that day.

Yesterday, I was at the Pentagon. In fact, I went in through the side of the Pentagon where American Airlines Flight 77 crashed into it. It is all rebuilt. It is strong, in fact stronger than ever. The reason I was at the Pentagon is the Secretary of the Navy, Secretary England, decided to name two new marine landing ships. They are named the USS Arlington, because that is where the Pentagon is and was hit, and Somerset after Somerset County, PA, to honor the victims of 9/11 who died in Pennsylvania and Virginia. These two ships will be a tangible demonstration of our shared resolve in this country. For our friends, neighbors, and loved ones who lost their lives, they will be fitting reminders of their sacrifice. ...

Tomorrow, we will be coming together, as is our tradition, to be cheering teams, grilling hamburgers and hot dogs, gathering around tables with those we love and those whom we cherish even more and, yes, indeed, we will pause. We will remember. We will never forget.

Three years after that terrible day that changed our lives, America has come back strong. Everything that makes us good is more appreciated than ever. We are resolved more than ever to stand strong for freedom. I am confident that with the wholesome character of our American people, justice will prevail and liberty will endure. ...

[Congressional Record: S9066]

"Let us take a moment to reflect upon the sacrifices of those who died on Takur Ghar, and on other remote battlefields in the war on terrorism. Let us rededicate ourselves to ensuring the safety of home and hearth for their families, and for ours. Finally, let the Senate and all Americans show deep gratitude for their unselfish decisions to step forward and say 'send me."

THE AMERICAN SOLDIER

March 19, 2003

Mr. President, I rise to honor our brave soldiers fighting in the global war on terrorism. We recently passed the first anniversary of Operation Anaconda, a critical seven-day military effort within Operation Enduring Freedom that helped break the back of the Taliban and al-Qaida in Afghanistan. It is fitting to take time to remember the sacrifice of the participants in that noble undertaking in the mountains of Afghanistan, and to ask Americans to pray for those who gave their lives. Let us also pause to recall the continuing efforts of our armed forces and civilian national security employees in Operation Enduring Freedom, and in the global war on terrorism. We are profoundly grateful for the sacrifices of all, and offer our prayers and deep gratitude to them and to their families.

On March 1, 2002, Americans went into battle near Gardez, Afghanistan, with Afghan and other allies, to attack al-Qaida and Taliban forces in eastern Afghanistan. Over the course of seven days, our forces engaged and defeated determined terrorist forces throughout mountains and rough terrain, at elevations as high as 12,000 feet, and in temperatures that dropped to 15 degrees Fahrenheit at night.

During Operation Anaconda, American Special Operations Forces combined with elements of the 101st Airborne Division, the 10th Mountain Division, and other aviation and ground units representing several allied nationalities to bring the war begun on September 11, 2001, directly to the terrorists and their supporters.

On March 4, 2002, a small American force came under night attack at a desolate mountain base at Takur Ghar. As a result of the ensuing engagement, seven Americans died. They gave their lives while trying to help each other, in a remote and forbidding place where their duty and their devotion to one another and their families had taken them. These seven Americans—like all Americans, civilian and uniformed, now engaged in the noble effort to end the terrorist threat to our Nation—were volunteers. They didn't have to be on Takur Ghar, but when called they did not hesitate to step forward and say "send me." As a testament to their heroism, at least eight Silver Stars, the Nation's second highest medal for valor, were awarded to participants in the battle along with almost thirty Bronze stars and numerous other awards.

Mr. President, Americans and their allies gave their lives during Operation Anaconda and elsewhere in Afghanistan. Americans and their allies have given their lives in other engagements in Operation Enduring Freedom.

Let us take a moment to reflect upon the sacrifices of those who died on Takur Ghar, and on other remote battlefields in the war on terrorism. Let us rededicate ourselves to ensuring the safety of home and hearth for their families, and for ours. Finally, let the Senate and all Americans show deep gratitude for their unselfish decisions to step forward and say "send me."

[Congressional Record: S3987-3988]

March 27, 2003

Mr. President, I take to the floor today to discuss the importance of acknowledging the tremendous risks and sacrifices our men and women in our Armed Forces make to ensure our continued freedom. In these turbulent and difficult times it is more important than ever to express our sincere and deep appreciation for the service of our Guard, Reserve, and active military.

To show our gratitude, I am pleased to announce that the first 7 days of June will be designated as Citizen Soldier Week. Through the passage of my resolution, S. Res. 58, we will recognize the unique sacrifices of members of the Reserves and National Guard.

Reserve and National Guard troops provide a substantial proportion of the combat forces required to carry out military operations. In doing so, many leave higher-paying jobs and place their civilian careers on hold to answer the call when our country needs their service. To begin providing the well-deserved recognition for their service, my colleagues and I have worked to make the first week of June, 2003, Citizen Soldier Week.

As I discuss this resolution and the importance of recognizing our citizen soldiers, I would like to make my colleagues aware of an active duty soldier, David S. Williams. David is a native of Chesapeake, VA who was captured by Iraqi forces after his AH-64 Apache attack helicopter was downed in central Iraq. I would like to offer my heartfelt concern and hope to David's family, and let them know I will do everything within my power to ensure David's safe return to his loved ones and his mother in Chesapeake, VA.

While David isn't a reservist or National Guardsman, his capture, and the effect it is having on his family and loved ones at home could happen to anyone who has the gumption to volunteer, serve, and defend our freedoms around the world.

And for that, all American soldiers—and their families—should be commended and thanked.

As our soldiers move closer and closer to Baghdad and continue to meet treacherous resistance, I believe it appropriate and right for the Senate to consider legislation to provide long overdue benefits to those who protect our cherished freedoms.

The Armed Forces Tax Fairness Act is an opportunity to provide our Armed Forces with logical tax relief to compensate them for their tireless and dangerous service to our country.

The men and women who join our military services are constantly faced with uprooting their families, being shipped off to foreign lands for months at a time, and long and difficult hours on the job. The jobs performed by our troops are often extremely demanding and come with great risk. As we are seeing daily in our liberation of the Iraqi people, these missions come with the real potential of casualties. While no legislation can compensate for the risks taken by our Armed Forces, I believe this legislation provides our troops deserved relief from unfair and burdensome tax.

The exclusion of tax from death gratuity payments should have been implemented generations ago. The freedoms that every American enjoys are protected by the service and sacrifice of those brave Americans who lost their life for this country. For the Federal Government to tax any portion of a death gratuity payment is wrong and insulting. The debt owed to the men and women who have died fighting for the principles of this country is incalculable, but the least this Government can do is offer the family some degree of comfort and compensation without asking for a portion in a tax return. Nothing can replace a soldier, sailor, airman or marine who does not come home; however, at least we can offer compensation without tax.

I fully support the Armed Forces Tax Fairness Act. However, I believe there are some other additional ideas that we, as the Senate, can adopt to improve the lives of those serving in our military. As many of my colleagues are aware, our troops are accorded a tax exclusion when serving in designated combat zones.

Earlier this year, I introduced legislation that would expand those combat zones to provide additional exclusion when our troops are deploying to dangerous areas around the globe.

I believe the combat zones tax exclusion should include the period in transit to that combat zone. By not subjecting military personnel to Federal or State taxes for this transit time, we would be providing a necessary benefit for the dangers associated with entering a combat zone. Deploying to a combat zone is a military operation that has its own set of dangers, from accidents to the constant threat of terrorist attack from the moment they leave their home port. And, our military personnel, including officers, should be covered by the full extent of the combat zone tax provisions during this critical period.

As we focus on the ongoing conflict in Iraq, I would like to remind my colleagues that we also have military personnel executing the war on terrorism. My legislation would also provide the proper tax breaks for service men and women serving on Operation Enduring Freedom in Guantanamo Bay, Cuba, and the Horn of Africa. We know that these two areas remain filled with danger and instability from terrorist threats, so the combat zone exclusion should also be applied to these duty stations.

Many of my constituents know the dangers associated with operating in Guantanamo Bay. The soldiers of the 2nd Battalion, 116th Infantry Regiment of the Virginia National Guard are serving in Cuba. They are playing an integral part in the war on terrorism and should be properly and fairly compensated for that service without taxation by the Federal Government during their service at Guantanamo.

I believe that personnel serving overseas in support of the global war on terror are performing duties at least as hazardous as those performed by personnel in some existing qualified hazardous duty areas.

As our Active, Guard and Reserve Armed Forces engage in a war with Iraq, while continuing our worldwide campaign against terrorism, it is vital that we do all we can to support the men and women who bear the burden of our defense and security. Passage of the Armed Forces Tax Fairness Act and the legislation I have introduced would further indicate to the brave men and women of the Armed Forces and their families that their service is of great value and their sacrifices are understood and appreciated by a grateful Nation.

[Congressional Record: S4508-4509]

" New technologies are being developed every day that can help save lives and improve the ability of our Government to fight and respond to terrorist threats. It is incumbent upon us as elected leaders to ensure our team, in fighting terrorism, is equipped with the best available and the most advanced technology. "

DEPARTMENT OF HOMELAND SECURITY

November 14, 2002

I believe the Department of Homeland Security proposal that we are now considering—the same one passed by the House last evening—preserves the essential functions outlined in the President's plan while also addressing several changes that will help ensure successful implementation.

Specifically, the new provisions clarify the roles and responsibilities of the Department and help form a top-notch workforce within the civil service framework. They also enhance research and development opportunities and protect civil liberties.

I am hopeful that my colleagues will come together and support this proposal as soon as possible. Let's get the job done. The job needs to get done without any further dilatory or political delays. Since September 11 of 2001, we have all seen the need to improve our homeland security. This matter has been debated for many months. As Senator Specter said—I will paraphrase him—as far as I am concerned, it has been fine-tuned to near perfection. It may not be 100 percent of what everybody wants, but 98 or 99 percent is pretty good work.

Madam President, as you may know, I am the chairman of the Republican high-tech task force, and I am very pleased to see that this proposal highlights the vital role technology and innovation play in our Nation's war to protect the people of our homeland from a variety of permutations of terrorism and terrorist threats.

This measure recognizes the importance of information technology and research and development in achieving the most effective homeland security.

There has been a lot of talk and a lot of focus on flow charts that talk about which department is here and which box goes here and this subagency there. All those flow charts are very interesting and relatively important, but most important is the flow of information, the ability of various Federal agencies to analyze the volumes of information and bits and facts and details—analyze all those thousands or tens of thousands of bits of information, analyze it, flag it, then act on it and, in some cases, also share that information within that Federal agency and also other Federal agencies, as well as State and local law enforcement agencies that also have a need to know that information.

New technologies are being developed every day that can help save lives and improve the ability of our Government to fight and respond to terrorist threats. It is incumbent upon us as elected leaders to ensure our team, in fighting terrorism, is equipped with the best available and the most advanced technology.

I have consistently maintained the Federal Government should and, indeed, must procure, adopt, and use these innovative technologies in an efficient and flexible manner in addressing this country's defense and homeland security needs.

I wish to briefly touch on a few of the important provisions I have worked on with representatives from the technology community and my colleagues in the Senate....

Let me highlight a few of the more salient provisions.

First, this proposal protects companies developing advanced technologies that help detect and prevent terrorism from assuming unlimited liabilities for claims arising from a terrorist strike. This provision helps ensure that effective antiterrorism technologies that meet stringent requirements are commercially available.

The reality is that without these safeguards, the threat of unlimited liability prevents leading technology companies from providing their best products to protect American citizens, American businesses, and governmental agencies.

The liability protections in this legislation are responsible to the Government, the industry, and also, very importantly, to the American taxpayer. I thank my colleague from Virginia, Senator Warner, for all his assistance, experience, and constructive leadership in this important aspect of the bill.

Second, along with Senator Bob Bennett of Utah, I am very pleased to see this legislation remove some of the legal barriers to information sharing between private industry and the Government. The threat to this country's critical information systems is extraordinary and this bill establishes procedures that encourage private industry to share infrastructure vulnerability information with the Government. The dialog between the Government and the private sector will ultimately help identify and correct weaknesses in our Nation's critical infrastructure while not compromising any of the provisions or protections provided under the Freedom of Information Act in other government agencies.

Information-sharing protections are particularly important in the area of cyber-security and threats. Taking preemptive measures to disclose vulnerabilities with the Government will help both the private and public sectors develop strategies to combat the numerous and constantly evolving cyber attacks threatening our Nation's critical infrastructure.

I encourage industry, law enforcement, and Federal officials to continue to work to build trust-based relationships and processes that will foster more information-sharing reporting.

Removing legal obstacles—which is what this bill does, which is very good—removing legal barriers to information sharing is very important and essential, but so is building trust.

A national forum on combating e-crime and cyber-terrorism was held at the Computer Sciences Corporation offices in Northern Virginia just 2 weeks ago by the Information Technology Association of America and the U.S. Attorney's Office for the Eastern District of Virginia where they brought together law enforcement and private sector leaders from all around the country to address some of the remaining obstacles to improving cooperation. These are the types of efforts I encourage, and I am hopeful this legislation will continue to promote.

Also included in the Thompson-Gramm amendment is the Federal Information Security Management Act, or FISMA, which will strengthen and protect the Federal Government's information and communications networks. FISMA establishes guidelines that are performance based. Let me repeat that. The guidelines are performance based so they can quickly adapt and respond to the fast-changing cyber-security threats. Strengthening the Government's information security is a vital component and piece of the homeland security puzzle. FISMA will foster accountability and make sure that every agency and department in our Federal Government prioritizes information security and promotes the use of commercially available technologies while avoiding technology-specific or product-specific government-wide security standards.

This is vitally important in making sure we get procurement that is good for the taxpayers and allowing all those who have great ideas to offer their programs, their systems, their products, and their efforts.

I am also happy to see this compromise proposal establishes a national technology guard or NET Guard. This is a bill that Senator Wyden and I introduced earlier this year to help local communities respond and recover from attacks on their information systems and communications networks.

After the September 11 attacks, I, along with other Senators, received volumes of information from numerous companies about their varied products, their systems, their programs, and their ideas regarding the defense of our homeland. As public servants, we want to be sure the Government has the necessary structure and process in place to test and apply new technologies to meet our homeland security needs.

The new Department of Homeland Security will have a designated center—and this is part of this bill—to serve as a technology clearinghouse to encourage and to support private sector solutions that enhance our homeland security.

Lastly, the Thompson-Gramm amendment makes the coordination of our Federal, State, and local officials charged with protecting our homeland a national priority. Over the last year, I have strongly advocated that any homeland security plan focus on interaction with local public safety officials as they are really on the front line of combating terrorist threats and attacks.

Specifically, I have worked in the Senate to promote the development at the local level of a voice and data interoperable communications system for Federal, State, and local emergency responders. Last year, this Congress appropriated $20 million for the CapWIN project. CapWIN has started to award contracts for the development of an interoperable communications system for Federal, State, and local public safety organizations in the greater Washington, DC area. That is Northern Virginia, the Maryland suburbs, and the District.

The CapWIN project is a real-life example of adapting technologies, specifically communications technologies, to address and overcome existing national security concerns, as well as homeland security concerns in this region.

I again thank my colleagues for listening to me, and to the tech community for their persistence and their positive leadership on this historic legislation. I respectfully urge all of my colleagues to support this carefully crafted measure that will help the President, Federal, State, and local agencies, and the private sector utilize the best innovations of technology, to analyze and respond and, thereby, protect the security of our American homeland.

[Congressional Record: S11014-11015]

"We all know that Saddam Hussein is a vile dictator with regard for only his own survival. He compromises the well-being of all Iraqis in his efforts to maintain power and accumulate wealth. History shows the Iraqi leader only responds when there is a gun put to his head. Sweet talking will not do any good with this man."

IRAQ

October 7, 2002

Madam President, I rise to address the most pressing and difficult issue facing our Nation today. Over the course of the next few days, we will be debating in the Senate and we will vote on the most serious responsibility the U.S. Constitution delegates to Congress, which is authorizing the use of military force against another nation.

I have only been here for about a year and a half. I passed in the hallway the senior Senator from Virginia, John Warner, who told me, "This is the first time you will have to do this." He said he has been through this experience seven times. I am sure he takes the same sort of care and consideration each time. But for me, this is the first time I have had to face such a question and such an issue as to where I stand.

It is my view the use of military force to resolve a dispute must be the last of all options for our Nation. Before entering into such a decision, it is absolutely necessary Government officials sincerely and honestly are confident they exhausted all practical and realistic diplomatic avenues and understand the short-term as well as the long-term ramifications and implications of such actions.

Exercising our best judgment based on the evidence of the threat, we must look at the consequence not only on the international community, but, more importantly, on the effect such action would have on the people of our country.

In considering the use of military action, my thoughts immediately turn to the people of the Commonwealth of Virginia. While the use of Armed Forces affects all Americans, it has traditionally had a significant impact on Virginia. The Commonwealth is home to literally tens of thousands of brave men and women who risk their lives to defend the freedoms we enjoy. The prospect of war places the lives of many of these men and women in jeopardy, and it means constant anxiety and fear for their families, wherever they may be based—whether in the U.S. or overseas, whether on land or on the seas.

I know from my experience as Governor how we rely heavily on the National Guard and Reserves whenever military action is necessitated, especially in the past decade. Military action will call up more Reserves and more of the National Guard when they are protecting our safety. It will disrupt those families and businesses and communities all across our great land.

This is not a decision I come to easily or without prayers for guidance and wisdom. The use of our Armed Forces means lives are at risk. The history of military action shows there are frequently unintended consequences and unseen dangers whenever the military is utilized. Fiscally, military action is expensive and can cause unrest both in the U.S. and international markets. When considering these outcomes, it is obvious using force to resolve the dispute is the least desirable and the last option for our country. But military action must remain an option for our diplomatic efforts to have any credibility or success.

I have listened and read comments from constituents and people all over this country, sincere words from the Religious Society of Friends and Pax Christi. They are well-meaning in pointing out their sentiments and the risks involved. However, we must weigh these risks and probable outcomes in the context of the threat Iraq poses to the U.S. and to our interests. I agree with the President, and the CIA, and the Department of Defense, and the State Department, that Iraq and Saddam Hussein's regime are a credible threat to the United States and our interests and our allies around the world. Because that threat is present and real, I believe the dangers will become substantially greater with continued inaction by the international community, or the United States acting in concert with allies.

The "whereas" clauses of the resolution we are debating effectively spell out good reasons, and reasons I look at for authorizing the President to use military action, if necessary. Saddam Hussein has continually, brazenly disregarded and defied resolutions and orders to disarm and discontinue his pursuit of the world's worst weapons. To bring an end to the Gulf War and Saddam's violent attempt to occupy Kuwait, the Iraqi leader unequivocally agreed to eliminate chemical, biological, and nuclear weapons programs, as well as putting severe limits on his missiles and the means to deliver and develop them. Since that armistice was reached in 1991, it has been consistently and constantly breached by Saddam's regime, and has not been enforced at all by the U.N. for the past 4 long years.

Can one imagine a nuclear weapon in the hands of Saddam Hussein? Let's not forget this is a head of state who has demonstrated his willingness to use chemical weapons on other nations and his own citizens with little or no reservation.

If the current Iraqi regime possessed a nuclear weapon, it would drastically alter a balance of power in an already explosive region of the world. Such a capability would renew Saddam's quest for regional dominance and leave many U.S. citizens, allies, and interests at great peril.

This man has no respect for international laws or rules of engagement. I share President Bush's fear that increased weapons capability would leave the fate of the Middle East in the hands of a tyrannical and very cruel dictator.

Most dangerous, currently, is not his desire to have nuclear weapons, but stockpiling of chemical weapons, the stockpiling of a variety of biological weapons; and also his missile range capabilities, that far exceed U.N. restrictions.

There is another concern not only that he has stockpiled biological and chemical weapons and the means of delivering them, but also the justifiable and understandable fear that he could transfer those biological or chemical agents to a terrorist group or other individuals. After all, Saddam Hussein is the same heartless person who offers $25,000 to families of children who commit suicide terrorist acts in Israel.

The goal of the United States and the international community needs to be disarmament. Saddam Hussein must be stripped of all capabilities to develop, manufacture, and stockpile these weapons of mass destruction, meaning chemical, biological agents, and the missiles and other means to deliver them by himself or by a terrorist subcontractor.

If regime change is collateral damage of disarmament, I do not believe there is anyone in the world who will mourn the loss of this deposed dictator. True disarmament can only be accomplished with inspection teams that have the ability to travel and investigate where they deem appropriate. To ensure they have full access to inspections is a key component of what the President of the United States is trying to get the United Nations to do.

We are trying to get full and unimpeded inspections. It would be appropriate for us to say noncompliance would result in forced disarmament.

The U.S. and the world cannot afford to have this mission undermined by wild goose chases and constant surreptitious, conniving evasion and large suspect areas being declared by Saddam to be immune from inspection.

I commend President Bush for recognizing the importance of including all countries in this effort. His statement to the United Nations on September 12, 2002, clearly and accurately spelled out the dangers Iraq poses to the world. By placing the onus on the United Nations, the President has given that international body the opportunity to re-establish its relevance in important world affairs, and finally enforce the resolutions that its Security Council has passed for the last eleven years.

Passing a new resolution will increase the credibility of the United Nations, which has steadily eroded since the mid 1990s. The Security Council has an obligation to provide weapons inspectors with the flexibility to accomplish their mission. This can only be realized if a resolution is passed with consequences for inaction or defiance.

That is why as the United Nations debates a new and stronger resolution against Iraq, the United States must be united in our resolve for disarmament. Passing a resolution authorizing our President to use military force in the event that diplomatic efforts are unsuccessful sends a clear message to the international community that Americans are united in our foreign policy.

I respectfully disagree with the premise that the President must first petition the United Nations before asking Congress for authority. I question: How can we expect the United Nations to act against Iraqi defiance if the U.S. Government does not stand with our President and our administration's efforts to persuade the United Nations and the international community to enforce their own resolutions?

It is right for us to debate the resolutions before the Senate, to voice concerns and sentiments in support or opposition. Each Member will take a stand and be accountable, and when the debate concludes, I respectfully ask my colleagues, when a resolution is agreed to, stand strong with our troops, our diplomats, and our mission. From time to time, one sees elected officials who moan in self-pity about having to make a tough decision that may not be popular. Well, I know the vast majority of the Senators, regardless of their ultimate position on this issue, can make tough decisions with minimal whimpering. Senators have all been elected by the people of their States to exercise judgment consistent with principles and promises.

As the Senate debates the merits of each resolution, it must be prepared for the possibility of continued inaction by the United Nations. Americans cannot stand by and cannot cede any authority or sovereignty to an international body when the lives and interests of U.S. citizens are involved.

I believe it would be a grave mistake for the United Nations to shirk its responsibility regarding Iraq; however, a consensus might not be reached with all nations on the U.N. Security Council. If that circumstance arises, the United States and the President will have a duty to garner as much international support as is realistically possible.

Blissful, delusional dawdling, wishful thinking, and doing nothing is not an option for the United States. However, continuing the diplomatic work in face of the Security Council veto is necessary not only for diplomacy, but to gain allies to help shoulder the logistical and operational burdens that would be a part of any military campaign.

It is true the United States can disarm Saddam Hussein alone. However, as we continue to pursue the venomous, vile al-Qaida terrorists and other terrorist supporters, we would greatly benefit from allied support in these extended efforts. I believe we will see more allies join this effort to disarm Saddam Hussein's regime. Britain will not be our sole teammate in this effort. As other countries begin to understand the severity of the threat, they will recognize it is in their best interest to disarm Iraq.

The UK along with Spain, Italy and some countries from the Middle East have supported our position. Kuwait, Qatar, and the Saudis have also indicated that maybe they will not send troops in, but have offered logistical bases that would be helpful for our tactical air strikes.

We do not want to make this a war against a particular group or certain religious beliefs. We must guard against any rhetoric or statement that is targeted against Muslims or Arabs. Our mission is to protect the United States, its allies, and interests by upholding internationally agreed-upon resolutions to disarm Iraq of biological, chemical, nuclear, and missile technologies. I urge the President to make absolutely clear that in the event we have to seek support from allies, that we continue to do so in the Middle East.

As a member of the Foreign Relations Committee, I have participated in committee meetings and top secret briefings and analyzed this issue very closely, and with questions. After reviewing the several resolutions offered by our colleagues, I believe the best way to provide the President with the authority and the support he may need is by passing the authorization for use of military force against Iraq.

This resolution, introduced and offered by Senator Warner and Senator Lieberman, as well as Senator McCain and others, gives the President the authority and flexibility to ensure the protection of the United States. I am particularly pleased that the resolution will task the President with determining that diplomatic means will not adequately protect the national security of the United States. This determination will ensure the United States is exhausting every diplomatic option before authorizing the use of our Armed Forces.

I refer to section 2 on page 7 of the resolution and those clauses therein: Where the Congress of the United States supports the efforts of the President to strictly enforce United Nations Security Council resolutions applicable to Iraq and encourages him in those efforts. It also encourages the President to obtain prompt and decisive action by the Security Council to ensure that Iraq abandons its strategy of delay, evasion, and noncompliance, and promptly and strictly complies with all relevant security resolutions.

I interpret this as also, in dealing not just with the United Nations, but also garnering allies in the process.

I will continue to listen intently to the debate on all the resolutions regarding Iraq. However, I truly and sincerely believe that Senate Joint Resolution 46, which I referenced earlier, will provide a sense of the Senate that the Congress, and most importantly, in our reflection in representation, a reflection that Americans are united behind our President and we support efforts to garner allied and U.N. support in the event that diplomatic options fail to disarm Saddam Hussein.

We all know that Saddam Hussein is a vile dictator with regard for only his own survival. He compromises the well-being of all Iraqis in his efforts to maintain power and accumulate wealth. History shows the Iraqi leader only responds when there is a gun put to his head. Sweet talking will not do any good with this man.

Now we are seeing this phenomenon play out as he allows weapons inspections to resume only after intense, consistent pressure from the international community. But even then what we are seeing again is the same shell game of conditions and prevarications that led to the departure of inspectors 4 years ago. We must not allow him to continue with these ploys of deception.

I do not believe any American welcomes the prospect of deploying our brave men and women for military action. However, standing strong and united as a country, together with our President, our diplomats, and our defense forces, and in favor of congressional authority to use force if it is absolutely necessary, is the best way to ensure Saddam Hussein is disarmed and military conflict is actually avoided.

The greatest responsibility of this Government and its officials is to protect and ensure the national security of the United States and our citizens. We know Saddam Hussein poses a threat to our country, and it is incumbent upon every Member of this body to help neutralize that threat. I am hopeful this problem will be resolved peacefully, through international diplomacy. But in the event those efforts fail, I do not want our President to be hobbled without the authority to protect the citizens of the United States of America.

Therefore, when my name is called, I will stand with President Bush, stand with our diplomats, stand with our troops and support this serious and necessary resolution, which is designed to save innocent American lives.

[Congressional Record: S10020-10022]